Southern Ghost Stories:
Opryland

Allen Sircy

Acknowledgements

There are so many people who helped me out along the way with this project. There were so many kind and generous people who were so friendly and accommodating to a guy who asked strange questions about ghosts in their workplace or residence.

I would like to thank the following people for their contributions:

Linda Bartee
Tara Bebber
Sonya Curtis Brinton
Melissa Brown
Laura Carrillo
Shawn Cook
Celeste Crim
Crystal Cruz
Juste Dylan
Eli Geery
Chantha Graves
Gemma Hardy
Amanee Harris

Lincoln Head
Jenny Hunt
Virginia McCabe
Scott Porter
Tiffany Sanchez
Marissa Shriner
Cathy Smith
Randy Smith
Emily Summers

Table of Contents

Introduction 4

Pennington's Bend 7

Two Rivers 13

Sacred Land 39

Birth of the Opry 41

Grand Ole Opry House 50

Roy Acuff House 66

Opryland 78

Opry Mills 139

Opryland Hotel 165

Music Valley Drive 185

Cursed 201

Introduction

Growing up in Nashville, I spent my summers at Opryland. My grandmother bought my sister and I a season pass every year, which was a blessing and a curse.

I was fortunate to have a grandmother who loved me enough to take me to the park once a week, but sadly she would have rather watched "I Hear America Singing" and other Opryland musical productions than ride "The Grizzly River Rampage". Even though I wasted a portion of my childhood sitting on benches watching shows instead of riding rides all day, I still always enjoyed my trip to the park.

Opryland was as big a part of my childhood as Star Wars, Hulk Hogan and G. I. Joe. It wasn't just a place. Opryland was an experience. When my Granny asked me if I wanted to go to Opryland, I would get a map of the park and methodically plan out the sequence in which I would ride the rides. I would look for theaters my grandmother would want to go to, just to see if it was close to a ride like the Flume Zoom or the Rock N' Roller Coaster. Despite my game plan of starting in the back of the park that was sure to be less crowded, I always gave in and rode the Flume Zoom first, since it was so close to the front gate.

When I became a teenager and started working, I didn't go to the park as much as I would've liked, but I still enjoyed it when I did go. Some of my favorite times weren't on the Wabash Cannonball or Chaos; they were with my cousin Matt riding back and forth on the Skyride. We talked and laughed as we watched the world go by from the top of the park. On more than one occasion I thought Matt was going to kill us because he thought it was funny when he got the cable car rocking back and forth.

I'll never forget where I was when I heard that the park was closing down. And like many Nashvillians, that feeling of disgust that still permeates through my bones. Some businessman in Texas didn't just decide to close down a theme park; he ripped away joy from my childhood that I will never be able to share with my son.

But enough of that, I'm sure you are here for the spooky stuff, not me ranting and raving about my childhood.

Back in 1995, I worked at the Opryland Hotel for several months in the Cascades American Café. One morning while on a break, I overheard two co-workers talking about "The Old Lady". According to hotel lore, the facility was haunted by an old woman dressed in white (or sometimes black) who had been spotted on occasion, usually in the Magnolia section of the property.

During my time as an employee, I never saw "The Old Lady" but every now and then I would hear co-workers talk about it. As I began to work on this project I talked with some people who had worked in the hotel, theme park, mall and the surrounding area. However, even though she had been known in my circles as "The Old Lady", I quickly found out that to others that had worked around Opryland, she was more commonly referred to as "Mrs. McGavock".

A ghost story about an old lady who haunts a hotel, theme park and mall doesn't make a lot of sense until you understand how she was betrayed after her death.

But there's more to Opryland than just an angry widow. Long before Opryland or Two Rivers, the entire area was at one point land that belonged to Native Americans.

The land we now associate with Opryland has quite the history. It's also very haunted. Let me tell you why…

Pennington's Bend

Long before there was Two Rivers, Opryland or Opry Mills there was McSpadden's Bend.

After the thirteen colonies declared their Independence from the British in 1776, the overmatched colonists needed an incentive to entice men to fight for independence against King George III and the mighty British army. In order to recruit new militia members, states such as Virginia and North Carolina issued bounty land. This incentive would be issued to veterans or their heirs once the war was over and the colonies prevailed.

The land grants served a dual purpose. While it served as an enticement to grow unsettled areas, which was populated mostly by hostile Native Americans at the time, it was also believed that by having skilled servicemen to defend those lands, it would encourage others to follow in settling in the area. With numerous battle-hardened individuals living in the new communities, Native Americans that were sympathetic to the Crown would be less likely to attack.

During this time, states like Virginia and North Carolina ceded much of their western land to the United States. Land in the western part of North Carolina would eventually become Tennessee.

One of the men who received granted land was Thomas C. McSpadden. In the mid-1780s McSpadden left Washington County, Virginia and cashed in his claim for land in middle Tennessee. A short time later McSpadden purchased more land along the large curve of the Cumberland River on the outskirts of Nashville. The former Virginia militia member operated a general store by the river where he traded with farmers and esteemed individuals like Andrew Jackson who also lived nearby.

After McSpadden's death his property along the Cumberland River was acquired by Graves Pennington. Pennington came to Nashville in the early 1800s and served in a local militia that was established to keep an eye on unfriendly Native Americans. For his services,

Pennington was awarded unclaimed land in middle Tennessee. After obtaining McSpadden's Bend, Pennington also began acquiring more land in the area and eventually established a 600 acre plantation that was maintained by 30-40 slaves. In addition to his plantation, Pennington was also an entrepreneur. He understood that he could make a lot of money offering settlers a way in and out of northeast Nashville and began operating a ferry across the Cumberland River. After Pennington's death in 1854, the property remained in the family for several years before it was purchased by Nicholas Coonrad. Though the ferry and plantation have been gone for almost 170 years, the area is still known today as "Pennington's Bend".

Like Thomas McSpadden, Nicholas Coonrad was also a veteran who saw opportunities in Tennessee. However, Coonrad was a shrewd businessman who typically bought land only to hold it for a while then sell it at a later date for a handsome price. This was the case for the land in Pennington's Bend. Coonrad held the land for almost ten years before he sold 640 acres to David Buchanan in 1794.

Hauntings

Tucked away in the northwest corner of Pennington Bend is Cock of the Walk, a popular restaurant that arguably serves up the best fried catfish in Nashville since 1985. It's thought that the establishment was built on land that at one time was part of the Pennington Plantation in the early 19th century. Today people that work in the building occasionally run into a "Lady in White" who is likely a member of the Pennington family.

"One night a young man was cleaning in that hallway going into the kitchen," explained Chantha Graves, the General Manager of the restaurant. "He came up to me and was white as a ghost. He asked me if anyone was in here beside us. I asked him if he saw something and he said that he might be seeing things, but he saw a girl in white wearing a bonnet. He said she wasn't from this time period. I said, 'Oh, you saw the ghost.' The next day he quit and didn't come back."

While I can't say for certain who the Lady in White is, I do know that Graves Pennington had a daughter named Amanda who died in 1857 at the age of 28. And according to Chantha that might line up with one of the spirits that are in the building. That's right. There's more than one.

"I think they were buried here," explained Chantha, who claims she can feel their presence. "We have a guy who comes in here and he sees them. There are two girls and a guy. They are dressed in white clothes from the 1800s and the girls wear a bonnet. I think they were in their teens and they are very protective of the area."

Oddly enough, the man also noticed that there were children running around in part of the restaurant that is known as "The Lee Greenwood Room". Naturally, this is close to where the young man also saw the Lady in White before quitting the next day. Servers have also watched as salt and pepper shakers jump off the tables in this part of the restaurant.

But it's not just Chantha and her associates that pick up on the spirits in the restaurant. Customers have noticed them as well. In fact, one customer snapped a picture of an upstairs window. She captured what appeared to be a small child playfully peeking out of the corner. Ironically enough, Chantha has had issues with the spirits in this part of the building too.

"The first day I started working there, I was going upstairs," explained Chantha. "As I started up the stairs I couldn't breathe. It was like something was sitting on my chest. I said there was something up there. One day I was sitting in my office by myself. I was alone and had locked the door and suddenly my office door started moving like someone was trying to come in. I scanned my camera around and no one was there. I've also been up there and it will feel like something is moving the furniture."

Things got so strange that Chantha spoke to her father about what was going on in the building. According to him, whatever was there was protective of the restaurant. Once she proved to them that she was there to take care of the place, it would leave her alone. And just like her father predicted, that has been the case. After getting off to a bumpy start four years ago, the spirits now leave her alone.

Two Rivers

The 1802 House

Roughly 25 yards away from the Two Rivers Mansion, just outside of Nashville, you will find a modest two and a half story brick house with seven rooms on the south side of the grounds. The house was built by David Buchanan but due to a massive debt the land and house was sold to John Arnold. A few years later, the property was acquired by Willie Barrow. Barrow was a local businessman who not only owned a plantation, but also served as the Justice of the Peace in Davidson County. Barrow named the property at the confluence of the Cumberland and Stones River "Belmont" and leased the land to farmers.

Sadly, after the War of 1812, the United States entered into a recession that devolved into a depression in 1819. The unexpected economic downturn sent the country spiraling into what became known as "The Panic of 1819". Barrow was greatly affected by the depression and had to sell Belmont to pay off his debts.

In 1819 William Harding acquired 476 acres of Barrow's fertile farmland at the junction of the Cumberland and Stones River to the south of Pennington's Bend. Harding came from a prominent family in middle Tennessee and his brother John founded the Belle Meade plantation in west Nashville. William acquired even more land over the next few years and eventually had over 1,100 acres and approximately 80 slaves. He called his property "Two Rivers Farm"and grew cotton, corn and raised livestock.

In 1830 William married Elizabeth Clopton, who like her husband also came from a prominent family in Tipton County, Tennessee. Despite a 23 year age difference, the couple was happy and in early 1832 Elizabeth became pregnant. Sadly, by mid-May, her 43 year old husband had died from bilious colic, which was caused by blockages in the gallbladder and liver from gallstones. When the young widow gave birth to a precious little girl four months later, she named her "William Elizabeth Harding". Though she was named in honor of her late father, everyone called her "Willie".

After William's death, Two Rivers was split into thirds. His wife Elizabeth received 1/3 of the property while the other 2/3 was set aside in a trust that was overseen by William's nephew, William Giles Harding of Belle Meade. After getting remarried, Elizabeth sold her share and the 1802 House to Joseph Clay who was related to her husband through marriage. In 1842 William Giles Harding bought the property and set it aside for Willie.

When Willie became of age she fell in love with her second cousin, David Harding McGavock. Like the Hardings, the McGavocks were a prominent family in middle Tennessee. Randal, David's cousin, served as the mayor of Nashville for a short time and owned the Carnton Plantation in Franklin, Tennessee.

Willie and David were married on May 23, 1850 in Memphis. With her mother already remarried, Willie inherited the 1,100 acre property in Nashville that had originally belonged to her father. The newlyweds lived with David's parents for a while before moving into the 1802 House a short time later.

Once the couple got settled in, David rebuilt Two Rivers Farm. With the help of approximately 50 enslaved men and women, David grew corn, grain and cotton and raised livestock on his 1,100+ acre orchard and farm.

With the plantation producing money hand over fist, Willie and David began building an opulent mansion in 1859. According to legend, the new home was designed by famous architect William Strickland. Strickland had designed the Tennessee State Capitol building in downtown Nashville. When Strickland passed away in 1854 as the house was being built, his son Francis stepped in and oversaw the project.

As the mansion was being built, Willie gave birth to a son, Frank Owen McGavock in 1851. Thirteen years later, Bessie McGavock was born. David and Willie raised the children in the old house while the new home was under construction.

Hauntings

Today the old house on the property is commonly known as "The 1802 House". The 1802 House is believed to be extremely haunted. In fact, in 2017 the daytime television talk show "Pickler & Ben" came to the house to film their Halloween episode. Hosts Kellie Pickler and Ben Aaron investigated the structure with acclaimed paranormal investigators Amy Bruni and Adam Berry from the hit TV show "Kindred Spirits" that airs on TLC. During the investigation Bruni and Berry used several different devices like a digital recorder and an SLS Kinect Camera that is used to detect the outline of a person.

According to Two Rivers Events Manager Laura Carrillo who accompanied the group in the house, it's believed that they made contact with a woman who had been beheaded.

"Supposedly it's a beheaded woman," said Carrillo. "We don't know if it was a murder or an accident. I was there watching and they were able to pick up an image on their box and an image came up beside Ben in the kitchen. It came up three feet off the ground and didn't have a head."

During the investigation the group began using a digital recorder and asked specific questions in hopes of eliciting a response. While Ben hammed it up for entertainment purposes and asked the spirit who their favorite Kardashian was, Kellie and the two seasoned ghost hunters began asking more pertinent questions, one of which got a very direct answer.

When asked if the spirit was a girl, a boy, a man or a woman; the group heard back through the digital recorder a very clear response that said, "A woman".

"We don't know if the woman was beheaded deliberately or it could've been an accident with a gun," explained Carrillo. "It involved the Buchanans or Abercrombies or the three people who owned it before William Harding owned it. There are 20 years that we don't know. There is definitely an entity of a woman who is beheaded."

But there's more to the 1802 House than the spirit of the woman who lost her head. The house has an effect on people and the temperature can vary drastically even in the dead of winter or the middle of the summertime.

"The 1802 House will make you feel horrible and nauseated," claimed Laura Carrillo. "There have been people who have tried to go in there and can't. The temperature can change too. I've opened it up and it's been 65 degrees in there in the middle of July. It's not a cold spot. The whole house is cold like it's the middle of January.

In 2018 the Travel Channel's Haunted Live filmed an episode in the Two Rivers Mansion and the 1802 House. According to paranormal investigator Scott Porter who starred in the show, they didn't get much activity during their time in the 1802 House, except for a rocking chair in the attic that rocked back and forth on its own.

"When we were there filming the house, we had a static camera set up there," recalled Porter. "We were watching it from outside and the rocking chair started rocking. All the doors were closed and none of the crew was in there. Because of the cameras you could see that there wasn't anyone in there."

After hearing Scott talk about his experience in the 1802 House I attended a paranormal investigation that was held on the property in November 2020.

Unfortunately during the investigation we only experienced a little activity in the 1802 House. After trying to make contact with the beheaded woman upstairs, I noticed a small spike on the EMF meter that detected changes in the magnetic field around it. However, downstairs Scott Porter got the biggest piece of evidence of the night. Earlier in the evening he had made contact with a little girl in the mansion using an app on his iPad called "Necrophonic". The app acts as a spirit box that allows the entities around it to use an internal sound box to form words to communicate.

Full disclosure: Before the investigation I had only heard about the app and had written it off as a cash grab by some app developer. However, after seeing it in action and hearing it form words that were intelligent responses, it made a believer out of me.

That night as we were downstairs in the 1802 House Scott began asking questions but wasn't having any luck in getting responses. But as we were wrapping up he asked if the spirit there was the person we had spoken to in the mansion earlier in the night. Almost immediately after Scott asked the question, a thundering "No" came booming out of the iPad.

Two Rivers Mansion

While construction on the mansion started in 1859, things came to an abrupt halt in February 1862 when the Federal Army seized Nashville. David McGavock, who was a staunch supporter of the Confederacy, was thrown in jail for ferrying Rebels across the Cumberland River. In addition to the stint in jail, he was also given a fine and the Union threatened to seize his farm and all his property unless he signed a loyalty oath. Realizing he was in a no-win situation, David swallowed his pride and signed the oath of allegiance to the Union.

Once the Civil War was over and life slowly got back to normal in middle Tennessee, the McGavocks stately red brick antebellum mansion with 28 rooms was finally completed in the 1870s. However, with no slaves to do the work, the farm began to fall on hard times and the McGavocks started selling portions of their land. To get by they also leased some of the farmland and buildings on the property to farmers as well as their former slaves.

As David and Willie struggled to keep things afloat, they were blindsided by the death of their five year old daughter Bessie. Willie especially took the death of their young daughter hard and threw herself into missionary work to keep busy. In fact, Willie served as Secretary of the Women's Board of Foreign Missions at the Methodist Episcopal Church and quietly donated diamond pins from her wedding veil to help purchase a school building in Shanghai, China.

In 1874 David and Willie's son Frank McGavock married Lula Spence and the two settled into Two Rivers. The following year the couple had their first child, Spencer. Six years later Frank and Lula had a little girl that was named "Willie" in honor of her grandmother. Unfortunately, the child lived to be eight months old before passing away in August 1881.

Death and tragedy seemed to always be lurking in the background in the mansion as the still-grieving Lula died five months later. As if things weren't sad enough around the old house, Frank Owen, Willie's stepfather who had come to stay with the family passed away a few weeks later in March 1882.

As David and Willie started to get older, Frank became more hands-on and took the reins at Two Rivers in the 1880s. By this time the farm had slightly rebounded and earned a reputation for raising thoroughbreds and having a large dairy farm. Unfortunately it wouldn't last. The collapse of two of the largest railroads in 1893 set off a downturn in the economy that almost ruined the McGavocks. After the death of Willie and David in the mid 1890s, Frank continued to lease farmland on the property in an effort to keep the family home.

However, still reeling from financial difficulties from the Panic of 1893 combined with gambling debts that David kept from his family that came to light after his death, Frank nearly lost the farm on more than one occasion. Somehow he managed to keep it in the family and pass it onto his son Spence before he passed away in 1920.

While Spence lived on the property and oversaw things, he was content to carve his own path and worked as a shoe salesman with the Nettleton Shoe Company in Nashville.

Mary Louise

After his father's death, Spence McGavock was in his fifties and had no children or heirs to pass the estate onto. In 1928, at the age of 56, Spence married his cousin, Mary Louise Bransford. Mary Louise was 50 years old and childless. She also just happened to be a distant cousin of her husband. Mary Louise had been married before but after a divorce early in her life, she had settled into life at Melrose, her parent's stately home in southeast Nashville. As a token of his love, Spence gave his new bride his grandparent's mansion as a wedding present. Mary Louise's father, William Bransford, who was a very wealthy man also wanted to give his daughter a gift and decided to pay to have the Two Rivers Mansion renovated and brought into the 20th century. His daughter was used to the finer things in life and couldn't possibly live in a home without electricity, steam heat, plumbing and modern bathrooms.

The newlyweds lived at Two Rivers for four years until the death of Mary Louise's mother, Manoah in 1932. At that point, the couple relocated to Melrose to care for her aging father who ultimately passed away eleven months later. After the death of William Bransford, Spence and Mary Louise returned to Two Rivers. Sadly, the couple wasn't able to enjoy the mansion very long. Spence dropped dead from a heart attack on the back veranda on December 4, 1936. After the death of her husband, Mary Louise once again moved back to Melrose.

Two Rivers sat empty for almost twenty years until Mary Louise sold Melrose and came back to Two Rivers for good in 1954. The McGavock widow made Two Rivers her home and lavishly furnished the mansion with pieces from England, France and Belgium. Mary Louise spared no expense bringing in extravagant wall paper, Persian rugs and expensive mirrors from New Orleans to freshen up Two Rivers. As she got older Mary Louise began having problems with arthritis in her hip and had an elevator installed in her husband's study so she could avoid the stairs.

On November 22, 1965 Mary Louise passed away and a modest funeral was held in the home the following day.

As an only child and with no children of her own, Mrs. McGavock left a very detailed will that was over 50 pages long. A portion of her jewelry was given to roughly 90 family and friends and a large sum of money was left to her servants. An expensive painting that hung in her home was willed to the Parthenon in Centennial Park. Mary Louise also established a $20,000 in a trust that was to be used to maintain her family's burial plots at Mt. Olivet Cemetery. After 20 years the remaining money went to a local church.

Mary Louise also donated a large tract of bottomland along the Cumberland River to her church. Her wishes were for it to be used for a school or an orphanage.

Her will also stated that a large portion of her estate was to be sold. The proceeds would go towards the expansion for the Division of Hematology at Vanderbilt Hospital and Medical School as well as a research fund that was named after her father.

On January 26, 1966 First American National Bank held an auction in Nashville to sell Mary Louise's remaining assets. Exquisite furniture, antiques, silver, vases, china, and 20 oriental rugs were just some of the items that were sold to the highest bidder. The highlight of the auction was a 46 ½ carat diamond pin that came from Mrs. McGavock's large jewelry collection.

On October 20 1966, Nashville Mayor Beverly Briley announced the city of Nashville had bought the Two Rivers Mansion as well as 460 acres for $995,000. The mansion would be preserved as a museum and set aside with 14 acres. The rest of the property would be developed and used for a greenway, skate park, golf course, water park, a school and the expansion of Briley Parkway.

Today Two Rivers Mansion serves the community as a popular wedding and events venue. Tours are offered during the summer on specific days. The historic home also holds events in conjunction with Halloween and Christmas. If you enjoy local history, it's worth your time to check it out.

Hauntings

Remember when I mentioned that Mary Louise left some land on the Cumberland River to her church to be used as an orphanage or school? Well, three years after her death the land was sold to National Life and Accident Insurance Company, the parent company of WSM. They would eventually build Opryland U. S. A. on Mrs. McGavock's property.

As you can imagine, this did not sit well with Mary Louise and it's believed to be the reason she has been spotted in not just Two Rivers, but all over her old land.

"The reason Mary Louise is unhappy is because of what happened with the Opryland complex," said Laura Carrillo, the Events Manager at Two Rivers Mansion. "Her wish was not granted. She has unfinished business and that's why she didn't cross over. That's why she's at the mansion, in the mall, hotel and was seen in the park."

If anyone would know, it's Laura. Not only has she worked in the historic mansion for thirty years, she also lived there for ten. During that time she has had a handful of odd experiences. In fact, late one night in the 1990s, Laura actually saw Mrs. McGavock inside her old home.

"I was closing up the house late one night," explained Laura. "I got to the back door and I heard something. I turned around and saw her in a white dress. It was a full apparition in the pocket doors in the front foyer. I blinked my eyes and it was gone. It was dark but there was enough light from the hallway for me to see her standing there. My heart stopped. It scared me but I haven't seen her since."

Just because Laura hasn't seen Mrs. McGavock lately, it doesn't mean she isn't there and doesn't make herself known from time to time.

"Working there for so long, things just go on," Laura said. "The doors will open. There will be no wind and it will open like something will come in and out. I've even seen the doorknob move. She also likes to play with the water. Sometimes you walk out of the bathroom. You've washed your hands and turned the water off like normal. Then you take two steps and the dual faucets are both wide open!

She also likes to play with electricity. She will turn lights on too. She loves to play with the chandelier. We do have issues with the alarm. One day I stepped outside and there was metro police. He said they had a report on the alarm. We were getting ready for an event and the alarm wasn't even on!"

Oddly enough, there is no rhyme or reason to Mrs. McGavock's mischievous behavior. When she decides to let you know she's around, she does it on her timetable.

"She makes her presence known but it's nothing really scary," continued Laura. "I've never had anything broken or anything like that. I know when she's there. I've tried to figure it out with birthdays, anniversaries and death dates but there's no pattern. It finally hit me and it depends on who is there or what is going on in the house. It's not like a light switch. You can't turn it on or turn it off. It's just antics.

Some people will hit the door and we'll immediately know. I've had a houseful of full blown gothic white witches and nothing will happen. Other people will come in, and all hell will break loose. The water will start running or you can't keep power on in certain rooms."

While Mrs. McGavock is harmless, she can be slightly mischievous at times. For instance, things in the mansion have a way of moving around on their own.

"I've had stuff taken," said Laura. "They will take it and stick it somewhere. You'll come back and your phone is gone. You'll think, 'I know I left my phone there', then an hour so later you will find it where it doesn't belong, somewhere else. One day I laid my watch down on my desk and got ready to leave for the day. When I went to get my watch, it wasn't there. Three months later I was down in the basement doing something, and there lies my watch in the middle of the floor!"

Mrs. McGavock doesn't just play tricks or mess with the people in the house. On the contrary, she's quite protective of the people who help keep up her home.

"The night of the tornado in 2020, I was living there," said Laura. "There was no power and it was completely dark. I was alone sleeping and it sounded like someone was throwing gravel at the windows on the north side of the house. It was a warning. I honestly feel like it was something trying to wake me up so I could go downstairs."

But it's not just Mrs. McGavock that keeps things interesting around the old mansion. The house is believed to be haunted by the spirit of children who like to play upstairs. The two playful entities are believed to be five year old Bessie and possibly Willie, Frank and Lula's young daughter that wasn't even a year old when she passed away.

The sound of children running around in the halls as well as a bouncing ball can sometimes be heard inside the house.

The spirit of a slave named Jack is also believed to also be inside the house. Jack typically appears when work is being done inside the house. While you can't necessarily see him, you are able to pick up a sour scent that resembles sweat and body odor.

It's not just Mary Louise, the girls and Jack in the old mansion. They also have a pet. That's right, according to those who have lived on the property a ghost dog has been spotted on numerous occasions around the grounds.

"When Mary Louise and Spence got married they were an older couple so they got a dog," explained Laura Carrillo. "I have a canceled check written to a kennel for an Alaskan Husky. He still appears around here on the back, on the south side of the house. Many people who have lived here have seen him. He makes no noise and has no collar on. He's kind of small to be a husky. I've seen it but it's been a long time. He doesn't make any noise or have any kind of aggression. He's just kind of there. Then you turn your head and he's gone. You never hear him bark or make any noise."

Growing up in the area, I had always heard stories about the Two Rivers Mansion. So when a paranormal investigation was held in 2020, I quickly signed up.

The event was hosted by Scott Porter from the Travel Channel's hit show, "Haunted Towns". That night we began in the parlors with an introduction and history of the property. Once that was done, we started the investigation there in the parlors. As we got started we almost instantly began interacting with a playful spirit that we believed was a child. Earlier in the night Scott had placed some little cat balls that lit up whenever they were touched in the middle of the floor. As we walked around them, none of them lit up. However, when you picked them up or moved them, you would see the little lights inside them go off. That night as Scott implored the spirit to touch them and play with them, the balls began to light up on several occasions.

After we watched the ghost interact with us and touch the balls, Scott pulled up the Necrophonic app on his iPad and began to ask the spirit what its name was. Oddly enough, as multiple people began to notice shadows moving around the parlors, we heard "Beth Ann" from Scott's device on two separate occasions. Someone in the room asked, "Are you a boy or a girl?" Almost instantly we heard, "I'm a girl" come from the iPad.

Eventually the trail went cold and we broke up into groups and went upstairs to various bedrooms to see if we could find some evidence in another part of the house.

When we got settled into one of the bedrooms upstairs we were greeted by an empath from Virginia who talked to us about things she had been feeling inside the house. After turning off the lights, she told us that she felt sadness in the room that revolved around children. At that moment she told us that she had a feeling that someone outside the room was watching us. Instantly, two or three people who were facing the closed bedroom door started shouting that there was a shadow moving underneath the door. Someone opened the door and looked into the hallway but no one was there.

Once everyone had calmed down, the empath passed around a digital recorder and we all took turns asking questions. When we played it back we began to hear our voices on the recorder. However, about halfway through the session, you could plainly hear a muffled voice say, "Stop." Needless to say, we had figured out that whatever was in the room with us didn't necessarily want to participate in our experiment and decided to move to a different room. And this is where the investigation took a really strange turn.

After we got settled into a different bedroom the empath asked if the house had played any part of the Civil War. I spoke up and told her that I didn't think it was used as a hospital like other historical homes in Nashville were.

She mentioned she was picking up the name "Jacob". I did a quick Google search on my phone and couldn't make any connections to anyone named Jacob to the mansion. Meanwhile, we passed around a digital recorder and asked questions hoping to get a response from whoever was in the house with us. Unlike in the other room, we didn't get any kind of response and the investigation sort of devolved into our group getting bored and making small talk. As we were talking, I noticed the empath had a strange look on her face like she was trying to solve a complicated math problem without a calculator. Out of the blue she asked if anyone knew what Goober Peas were. I pulled my phone back out and did another Google search. Sure enough, the top search result was a YouTube video called "Goober Peas" so I played it.

Once the video started playing it became apparent that the song was something the Confederate Army would've marched to during the war. I asked the empath why she asked about the song and she shrugged her shoulders. She told us that it just popped into her head and that she had never heard it before.

Thinking that perhaps we had a soldier in the room with us, I pulled up *Dixie* on YouTube and played it to see if I could get a response. Instantly, a REM-pod, a piece of equipment that measures temperature and changes in its small magnetic field located in the hall, started going off.

After the song ended, I played it again. This time the REM-pod stopped and my EMF meter that is used to pick up electromagnetic anomalies started to light up.

A few months after the investigation I talked to Laura Carrillo about the "Goober Peas incident" and told her that we thought a soldier might have been upstairs with us. Laura quickly shot me down and informed me that soldiers were not at the mansion during the war. According to her, it was nothing more than the little girls upstairs just liking the music.

Sacred Land

Before I can tell the rest of the stories, I really have to go back, way back before the Hardings, McGavocks, Penningtons or even Buchanans lived in the area.

In the 1300 and 1400s much of middle Tennessee was home to Mississippian Period Indian settlements. And given the proximity to the Cumberland River, it is no surprise that Native Americans would've lived and hunted along the water. But as the white man began moving west in the 19th century, most of the Native Americans were flushed out of the area and their burying grounds were lost to time until the land was developed and homes were built. One of the first to discover the remains was Judge John Overton who bought some land 15 miles south of Two Rivers. When Overton was building his home, slaves unearthed over 30 stone box graves containing the remains of Native Americans as well as offerings of pottery, utensils, primitive jewelry, water bottles, and rattles.

After the shocking discovery Overton named his home "Golgotha", which means "Home of the Skull." However, after Overton got married and began teaching law in home he gave his home a much friendlier name, "Traveler's Rest".

In the 1940s crews building a subdivision near Breeze Hill in South Nashville made an astonishing discovery. The workers accidently stumbled across a burying ground containing the remains of over 3,000 Native Americans. Experts were brought in and the land was preserved as a park and the new subdivision was scrapped.

A smaller Native American burying ground was discovered along Stones River, less than a mile away from Two Rivers Mansion in the mid-1800s. The burying ground consisted of a number of mounds that contained tombs and stone box graves. While plowing a road through the area, David McGavock unearthed 50 to 100 graves. David also discovered a tomb that looked like it contained the remains of a chief and his wife. Both had been buried with decorative shells over their mouths and the chief had been holding two long clubs made from stone.

While David donated the decorative shells to the Tennessee Historical Society, the clubs were given to his children to play with and a number of the skulls that he dug up were placed on the stakes of a fence on the property.

In October 1971 while Two Rivers Golf Course was being constructed a half mile away from the mansion, a crew discovered another long-forgotten Native American cemetery. While leveling out the land to build the eighth, tenth and eleventh fairways, workers from Metro Parks inadvertently dug up burial mounds that contained over 20 stone box graves and a number of artifacts. Work was halted and the remains were exhumed and relocated. One of the skeletons was put on display in the library of nearby McGavock High School.

Birth of the Opry

In 1900 Nashville businessman C. A. Craig bought the floundering National Sick and Accident Association. To turn things around the company expanded their operations and began selling life insurance policies. Business quickly picked up and the company slowly branched out of middle Tennessee and into the rest of the United States.

During the early 20th century, the main way to advertise your business was by radio or newspaper advertising. Instead of paying a fortune for radio spots around the country, C. A. Craig decided to invest in a 1,000 watt 6A Western Electric transmitter and built his own radio station in a small office on the seventh floor of the National Life building.

To name their new radio station, National Life officials harkened back to their motto, "We Shield Millions" and WSM was born.

To celebrate the first broadcast of WSM, National Life officials set up a public address system around their headquarters at the corner of 7th and Union so locals could hear the broadcast. With hundreds of people standing in the streets, Edwin W. Craig, a Vice President with the company (and C. A.'s son), went live over the air on October 5, 1925. Edwin proudly introduced the station by saying, "This is station WSM. We Shield Millions, owned and operated by the National Life and Accident Insurance Company, Nashville, Tennessee.

Dr. George Stoves from the West End Methodist Church was then introduced over the air. Stoves delivered a prayer which was followed by the playing of the national anthem. The Al Menah Shrine Band, who had set up on the roof of the building performed a stirring rendition of *The Star Spangled Banner*. Edwin Craig then introduced his father, WSM President C. A. Craig. The elder Craig gave a short speech about National Life and WSM before turning the microphone over to Tennessee Governor Austin Peay and Nashville Mayor Hilary E. Howse. Both politicians said some words and Lambdin Kay, a radio personality from WSB in Atlanta known as "The Little Colonel" took over the broadcast.

During the Little Colonel's portion of the show, the audience was treated to performances by Beasley Smith and Francis Craig Orchestra followed by the Fisk Jubilee Chorus and Joseph McPherson from the Future Metropolitan Opera. Other radio stars like "The Merry Old Chief" Leo Fitzpatrick, from WDAF in Kansas City and "The Solemn Old Judge" George D. Hay, from WMC in Memphis were also brought in to keep things moving along that night.

At 9 PM George D. Hay took the microphone and blew into his signature steamboat whistle before introducing the Knights of Columbus quartet who was followed by Aleda Waggoner and Vincent Kuhn.

From midnight to 2 AM, as a precursor for what was to come, Jack Keefe took over the broadcast and presided over a portion of the show called, "The Grand Jamboree." The Grand Jamboree featured Bonnie Barnhardt, Joe Combs and a few other local performers.

After the inaugural broadcast, WSM began broadcasting on Monday, Wednesday, Saturday and Sunday nights. The station featured live music provided mostly from local orchestras. Two days after the station went on the air, the audience was treated to the 1925 World Series. Local baseball fans were thrilled to hear the action, especially when the Pittsburgh Pirates overcame a 3 to 1 game deficit to defeat the Washington Senators in a best of seven series.

George D. Hay

In late November George D. Hay was hired by WSM and brought in to oversee the programming. "The Solemn Old Judge" began to tinker with the format and wanted to mix things up slightly from the classical orchestra-style music that was predominantly featured.

In 1918, while working as a reporter in Memphis, Hay had been assigned to cover the death of a Missouri soldier who died during World War 1. After the serviceman's funeral, Hay was invited by some locals to come listen to some live music across the state line in Mammoth Spring, Arkansas. Not having anything better to do, the curious reporter tagged along and made his way to a small cabin in the middle of nowhere. To his astonishment, Hay discovered dozens of people packed into the tiny building singing and dancing along as an old man played the fiddle.

That hoedown in Arkansas always stuck with "The Solemn Old Judge" and he wanted to see if the mountain music he enjoyed that night as a reporter would resonate with audiences on WSM. In late November 1925, a local fiddler named Uncle Jimmy Thompson was brought in to play for an hour to test the waters. When Hay began to get feedback from the new program he found that WSM listeners didn't like it. They loved it! The new sound was such a hit that WSM began broadcasting a new program called "Barn Dance" the following month.

The new show was so popular that people didn't just tune in at home; they also came to the National Life building and listened in the hallways as live bands played bluegrass and Appalachian-style music in the small studio. As the crowds grew and started to become a safety and fire hazard, WSM officials moved to another studio called "Studio B", then eventually to a 500 seat auditorium on the seventh floor called "Studio C".

Barn Dance was inadvertently renamed in 1927 when Hay made a remark about the preceding show having played music from the "Grand Opera". Not missing a beat, "The Solemn Old Judge" boasted that he would be featuring music, "from the Grand Ole Opry!"

That same year WSM expanded their footprint by increasing the station's power to 5,000 watts. Five years later, the signal was increased to 50,000 watts when an 878 foot tower was erected along Concord Road in Brentwood, Tennessee.

At that time, the WSM tower was the largest in the world. As landline telephones grew in popularity in the mid-20th century, those that lived near the tower began hearing WSM programming every time they picked up the phone! WSM worked with the telephone companies to have special filters installed on the  telephones so locals could use them without any issues.

As the Grand Ole Opry grew in popularity, National Life executives began to have problems with overzealous fans that came to watch the show. Not only were they overflowing into the halls, but they began to wander around the National Life offices too. One day after an executive couldn't get into his office due to all the fans in the building, it was decided that the show had gotten too big and it had to be moved to a bigger venue off-site.

In 1934 the Opry moved to the Hillsboro Theatre on the corner of Hillsboro and Acklen. The Hillsboro Theatre was a silent movie house that at the time was the nicest venue in Nashville. Even with 800 leather-covered seats and the largest stage in middle Tennessee, WSM officials still made the Grand Ole Opry free to attend. The Opry was still red hot and to make it so more people could enjoy the Opry, WSM tweaked their format and began running two shows instead of one. Before the Opry moved to the Hillsboro Theatre, artists typically played a 30 minute set. With the new format, the performers would play for 15 minutes in the first show and another 15 minutes in a second show. WSM also broke up the show into segments and sold advertising for different parts of the radio broadcast. The change in format worked so well that the Opry brass kept it that way going forward.

In 1936 WSM moved the Grand Ole Opry to the Dixie Tabernacle on Fatherland Street in East Nashville. The religious meeting hall held 3,500 people but wasn't quite as comfortable as the posh Hillsboro Theatre. Even though fans sat on wooden benches set up on a dirt floor, the people still crammed into the building to see their favorite Opry stars perform live on stage. However, to attend the show you had to have a ticket. To get a ticket you had to interact with employees of National Life who were in charge of distributing them. This was an effective sales strategy by the company to engage and interact with potential future customers.

Three years later the Opry moved once again, but this time it was to the elegant 2,200 seat War Memorial Auditorium in downtown Nashville. At the time, War Memorial was considered to be the premier concert and events center in Nashville and WSM began charging fans 25 cents to get in to see the show. Unfortunately, the rowdy Opry fans proved to be too much for the upscale venue. In 1943 War Memorial officials politely asked WSM to find a new place for the show.

On June 5, 1943 the Opry moved to the Ryman Auditorium on Fifth Avenue. The building had been originally built to host religious gatherings in 1892. But as the building entered the 20th century, it began hosting lectures, concerts and even boxing matches to pay the bills

During its time at the Ryman, the Grand Ole Opry gradually changed. WSM went from featuring string bands and banjo players to building the broadcasts around entertainers with personalities like Roy Acuff, Uncle Dave Macon and Minnie Pearl. In fact, a young Elvis Presley even played the Opry in 1954.

In honor of Bill Monroe, the Opry member and songwriter of the bluegrass classic *Blue Moon of Kentucky*, the future King of Rock n Roll played the song during his set on the show. Despite an abundance of cheers from the audience and a thumbs up from Bill Monroe, Jim Denny, the man in charge of booking the show, didn't approve. Elvis Presley and his over the top rockabilly music were not welcome at the Grand Ole Opry. At the end of the night Denny advised the teenage singer from Memphis to go back home and pursue a career as a truck driver.

The Ryman Auditorium was home to the Opry for 31 years. During that time, the old house of worship became known as "The Mother Church of Country Music", a title that it still proudly holds today.

Grand Ole Opry House

In the early 1970s WSM officials were becoming increasingly frustrated with the Ryman Auditorium. As the Grand Ole Opry grew, the old building that was originally built as a house of worship in the 1890s had become too small for the popular radio show. And worst of all, there was no air conditioning!

Officials hired renowned architectural firm Welton Becket & Associates to work on designing a new Grand Ole Opry House. After completing their work on the Contemporary Resort in Walt Disney World, the firm got to work designing not only a live music venue, but also the world's largest radio and television broadcasting facility.

The plan for the Opry's new home was to place it next to the Opryland theme park that was still under construction along the Cumberland River. The new 147,270 square foot Grand Ole Opry House would be able to hold 4,350, which was double the size of the Ryman. In addition to more seating capacity, the new venue would have unrivaled acoustics, state of the art lighting, modern recording equipment and most importantly, more space for the bands, comedians and other entertainers that performed on the Opry. The new venue would have a large area for staging and rehearsing as well as 14 lavish dressing areas and a lounge.

The stage was designed as a semicircle that thrust out into the auditorium. With this feature, the artist could get closer to the audience during their performance on the Grand Ole Opry. The fan experience was important to WSM and Opry officials wanted to make sure the new Opry House was more fan-friendly than the Ryman Auditorium. The old venue had a hundred or so seats with blind spots due to pillars and posts that prohibited fans from seeing the entire stage. The new Opry House wouldn't just have unobstructed views in every seat, there would be a large area down front for fans to snap a picture of their favorite performer on stage.

The most important feature of the Opry House's stage wasn't new. In fact, it was actually an old one. In order to tie the radio show's present and future to its past, Opry officials decided to cut an eight foot square from the Ryman stage. The oak and maple boards scuffed by the boots of legendary artists Elvis Presley and Hank Williams were carefully carved into a six foot circle and placed into the center of the stage at the new Opry House. Opry legend Roy Acuff tried to persuade officials to paint a picture of the Ryman Auditorium in the circle but was overruled by WSM.

In addition to the main stage and auditorium at the Grand Ole Opry House, a smaller studio called "Studio A" was also built onsite. A separate 90 x 80 square foot studio with a balcony was constructed inside the building. Over the years, shows like "Hee Haw", "Primetime Country" and other nationally syndicated radio and television shows have been recorded in Studio A.

Grand Opening

On March 16, 1974 WSM went live from the new Grand Ole Opry House. Of the 62 Opry members, 50 of them were on hand for the festivities. From Roy Acuff to Minnie Pearl, the show featured a who's who of country music. But the biggest star that night wasn't even a singer or entertainer. An amateur piano player who just happened to be the 37th President of the United States was on hand for the dedication of the brand new Opry House.

Richard Nixon, who by this time was knee-deep in the Watergate scandal, flew in from Washington D. C. to attend the Opry. His wife Pat, who was celebrating her 62nd birthday, flew into Nashville from South America to meet her husband at the show.

Security was usually pretty tight at the Opry, but that evening things were locked down by Secret Service agents. Security was so strict that Roy Acuff was turned away when he arrived at the Opry House that afternoon. Acuff tried to plead his case with a member of Nixon's security detail but was once again denied entry. Fortunately for the singer, another secret service agent recognized "The King of Country Music" and allowed him to enter the building.

That night at the Opry, Roy Acuff introduced Richard Nixon to start the show. As the house band played a country music version of *Hail to the Chief,* Nixon came onto the stage along with his wife, actress Dorothy Ritter and NLT Board Chairman William C. Weaver.

The President walked over to the microphone at the center of the stage and pulled out a yellow yo-yo from his coat pocket. Taking a jab at Acuff who was a wiz with the toy, America's Chief Executive said, "I haven't learned to use this thing yet." As the audience laughed, Acuff then prompted the Commander in Chief to play "Happy Birthday" on the piano for his wife.

Ever the showman, the President not only played the song for his wife, but he also did an encore and performed "My Wild Irish Rose" with the house band. After Nixon brought down the house, Acuff asked him to help unveil a plaque commemorating the special occasion. Not missing a beat after the ceremony was over Nixon quipped, "It must be time for a commercial."

After the break, Acuff once again introduced the President. Nixon, who was a country music fan, gave a speech about the importance of country music followed by a bit where the country legend attempted to teach the clumsy President how to use the yo-yo. As the Commander in Chief struggled to get the hang of it, he joked, "I'll stay here and learn to yo-yo, and you go to Washington and be the President."

After another break, Roy Acuff prodded the President to join him in the center of the stage. Nixon, who was sitting on the stage next to his wife, got up and began walking toward Acuff until he asked him to play the piano again. The President playfully said, "Whoa!" then turned around and walked back to his seat. As the crowd chuckled, Nixon walked over to Acuff and put his arm around him as they hammed it up with him for a few moments. As the two men talked onstage, the Commander in Chief noticed that he wasn't in front of a microphone. He casually slid over to the closest one and began talking about the history of the song, *God Bless America*.

With the crowd firmly in his back pocket, Richard Nixon brought down the house one more time by playing "God Bless America" on the piano. When the President was done playing, he walked over to his wife and exited the stage as the house band played their hillbilly version of *Hail to the Chief*.

God Bless the USA

Six years after Richard Nixon played the Opry, Jimmy Carter, the 39th President of the United States attended a town hall-style fundraiser at the Grand Ole Opry House for his re-election campaign. Though he was a sitting President, Carter was in a dogfight with popular actor-turned California Governor, Ronald Reagan for the Presidency. By holding a large fundraiser at the Opry just a few weeks before the election, Carter was hoping to steal some swing voters in a Republican state while raking in some much needed cash for the campaign down the stretch.

Hank Snow, Bill Monroe, June Carter Cash as well as dozens of Opry members were on hand for the event. Conspicuous by his absence was June's husband, Johnny Cash. Cash was said to be out of town filming a movie, but it wasn't much of a secret that the "Man in Black" detested politics. Even though he couldn't be there with his wife, Johnny paid for a banner that hung up in the Opry House that said, "God bless you Mr. President."

The fundraiser was a resounding success for the Carter re-election campaign. The President raised $100,000 from hundreds of supporters who paid at least $500 to attend the event. While President Carter didn't do any tricks with a yo-yo, he did accompany the Carter family on stage and sang with them while they performed their classic song *Will the Circle Be Unbroken.*

Ultimately Carter lost his bid for re-election and was soundly defeated by Ronald Reagan.

In 1984 President Reagan came to Nashville to wish Roy Acuff "a happy 42nd anniversary of his 39th birthday" along with 4,000 Republicans who had been invited to attend.

After joking around with Acuff about his 81st birthday, the President made some remarks about Barbara Mandrell, who had recently been in a serious car accident. Ever a politician, Reagan then began playing to the crowd and gave a speech about how wonderful Nashville was. He got back to his friend Roy Acuff and joked about the singer's popularity during World War II. According to the President, when the Japanese would attack, they'd yell, "To hell with Roosevelt, to hell with Babe Ruth and to hell with Roy Acuff!" Reagan concluded his birthday greeting to "The King of Country Music" by saying, "Long live the King!"

But with the Presidential election coming up in two months, Reagan circled back and asked the crowd, "Do you feel better off than did four years ago?" Reagan then railed on his opponent Walter Mondale's campaign promises and joked about how they were similar to Minnie Pearl's hat and the "big price tags hanging from them." Reagan continued with the playful barbs and explained that the left couldn't play the Opry, "because all they do is sing the blues." The President continued to zing his opponents until he wrapped things up by singing *Happy Birthday* with the crowd.

And just when you thought the night was over, a seven foot tall birthday cake was brought onstage. Billy Walker, Chet Atkins and other Opry stars also came out with Minnie Pearl as she introduced Lee Greenwood. Greenwood, who had recently released the song *God Bless the U. S. A.*, walked onto the stage and began singing the now classic song as the President clapped and sang along. With streamers and confetti filling the air (and covering the oversized birthday cake) Roy Acuff thanked everyone for coming and the show came to a close.

Reagan's successor, George H. W. Bush visited the Opry House several times during his years as Vice President as well as when he was the Commander in Chief. In 1991 Bush was on hand for the CMA Awards that were held in the Opry House. While the 41st President didn't twirl a yo-yo or give a speech, he did sit quietly and watch the show with the First Lady. After winning the prestigious Entertainer of the Year award Garth Brooks took a moment to thank some of his biggest influences, "the Georges". Garth apologized to George Bush, and recognized country music legends George Jones and George Strait for what they meant to him and his career. The Commander in Chief laughed it off and stuck around after the show to mingle with the entertainers.

Over the years other notable politicians have gravitated to the Opry House. In fact, First Lady Rosalynn Carter Opry House in the mid-1970s while fundraising in Nashville.

Most recently Joe Biden visited the Opry House in 2010 during a visit to Nashville. While touring the venue the former Vice President jokingly assured reporters he wasn't going to sing.

In addition to prominent politicians and government officials, rock and roll and R&B stars like James Brown, Pharrell Williams, The Eagles, Chris Isaak and George Thorogood have also performed at the Opry House over the years. Even acclaimed actors Dennis Quaid, Kevin Bacon and Kevin Costner have also performed with their bands in the historic country music venue.

Will The Circle Be Unbroken?

On May 1, 2010 with rain pouring down all over Nashville, Grand Ole Opry officials became alarmed at the water that was spilling over the banks of the Cumberland River. As water began to fill into the home of the Opry, quick thinking staff members began moving instruments and other historical items from the Opry museum to safer areas.

By May 3rd the heart and soul of country music was submerged in four to ten feet of water. Pews were ruined, the big red curtain had been destroyed, lights were caked with mud and the floors were a total waste. But the circle? It was under two feet of water and soggy. Yet, it was still unbroken.

Bent, but not broken, the Grand Ole Opry didn't cancel a single show. The Opry moved to downtown Nashville and bounced around to the War Memorial Auditorium and its old home, the Ryman Auditorium for the rest of the summer.

WSM and their parent company Gaylord spent $20 million to renovate the Opry House and to get it back up and running as quickly as possible. For nearly five months crews worked diligently on restoring the Grand Ole Opry House to its former glory while also updating the dressing rooms. On August 25, 2010 Opry members Brad Paisley and Little Jimmy Dickens were on hand alongside former Nashville Mayor Karl Dean as a crew returned the newly refurbished six foot wooden circle back into the Grand Ole Opry stage.

After the disastrous flood earlier in the year, the Grand Ole Opry House grand re-opening took place on September 28, 2010 with a special concert called "Country Comes Home". The show featured Brad Paisley, Keith Urban, Diamond Rio, Dierks Bentley, Blake Shelton and many other notable country stars who wanted to be there for the special occasion.

After a video montage played, dozens of notable performers and legends like Martina McBride, Marty Stuart, and Charlie Daniels joined Brad Paisley and Little Jimmy Dickens onstage to sing *Will the Circle Be Unbroken*. That night after performing their hit song, *Hillbilly Bone*, Trace Adkins surprised Blake Shelton and asked him to join the Opry. Overwhelmed with joy, Shelton hugged his duet partner and accepted the invitation.

The Grand Ole Opry is broadcast live from the Grand Ole Opry House on Tuesday, Friday and Saturday nights. You can also take backstage tours of the venue from each day for a nominal fee. The tours take you behind the scenes of the Opry and you get to see things like the member's mailboxes and the lavish dressing rooms that the performers use before and after their performances.

Most importantly, when you take the backstage tours, you are allowed to have your picture made standing in the historical circle that thousands of performers have stood in over the years.

Hauntings

Like other buildings in the area, the Grand Ole Opry House is said to be haunted by the spirit of Mrs. McGavock. Opry House staff members and security officers have claimed to see the spirit of a woman in a black dress from time to time. According to those who have been in the building late at night, Lady McGavock has been spotted on the Opry stage as well as roaming around in the lobby.

But you might be surprised to learn that Mrs. McGavock isn't the only entity in the Opry House. Apparently there is also someone wearing cowboy boots that makes his presence known not just on stage, but next door at the Roy Acuff House too.

"A few years ago we had a blackout," recalled an Opry House security guard. "Because of the blackout one of us had to be in the building at all times.

I was sitting on the fifth row when a female security guard in the Acuff House called me around 1 AM in the morning. She was in a total panic saying she kept hearing doors closing and wanted me to come over there. I told her I'd meet her out front. Well, as I was sitting there it sounded like someone started walking across the stage in cowboy boots. I heard it as clear as a bell.

There are a lot of things like that happen. They say it's Lady McGavock. I hadn't seen her, but they say she walks around all over the place."

Roy Acuff House

In 1903 Roy Acuff was born in the small town of
Maynardsville, in east Tennessee. Roy's father, Neil Acuff
was an important man in his community, serving as both
a Baptist preacher and an attorney who would later
become a judge. Neil also prided himself as an amateur
fiddle player. Like his dad, Roy loved music as well and
even sang in the church choir as a child. However, like
most boys, Roy loved playing sports. In high school he
was regarded as a gifted athlete who lettered in several
different sports like baseball, basketball and football. As
Roy got older he put music on the backburner and began
pursuing his dream of playing professional baseball.

After graduating high school, Roy began playing baseball
for a city league team. Playing shortstop and the outfield,

Roy turned a lot of heads and even got the attention of baseball scouts from the New York Yankees. Wanting to evaluate the young prospect's skills, the scouts arranged for a tryout just to see if Roy Acuff had what it took to play in the major leagues. In the meantime, Roy had arranged to go on a fishing trip to Florida with a friend. Unfortunately for Roy, he was out in the sun way too long and came down with a case of sunstroke. Sunburned and sore, Roy was undeterred. He went back home to Knoxville and did what he always did, play baseball to stay sharp for the Yankees.

One scorching hot summer afternoon Roy ran into the dugout in between innings. As he stood there talking to teammates, the twenty five year old ball player passed out and fell helplessly to the ground. With his arms and legs cramping, Roy was rushed to the hospital where he was diagnosed with sunstroke.

Roy was eventually sent home and advised by doctors to take it easy for a few weeks. However, with a tryout with the Yankees on the horizon, the young prospect knew he needed to get out of bed and back to the baseball diamond. Unfortunately as soon as Roy hopped out of bed, he passed out and fell straight to the floor. After falling three more times, Roy began to realize his dreams of playing professional baseball were over. In fact, in 1930 Roy spent the majority of the year in bed.

While trying to recover Roy began playing with a new toy called the yo-yo. Since he could no longer play baseball, Roy spent countless hours mastering the new contraption that was hugely popular at the time. In addition to his newfound skill with the yo-yo, Roy also began to listen to bluegrass music and became intrigued with his father's fiddle. The former baseball player began stroking the fiddle with a bow as he listened to the musicians on the records. Slowly but surely, Roy started to pick things up and started to play what he had heard by ear.

After his health had improved, word got around that Roy was quite the fiddle player. A local man who went by the name Doc Hauer recruited the former baseball prospect to be a member of his traveling medicine show that featured music and comedy. The group played small venues in the mountains of east Tennessee and Virginia. Roy and the traveling ensemble played to hundreds, or sometimes thousands of people before Doc Hauer would take center stage to pitch a tonic that he claimed could cure a variety of ailments.

In 1934 Roy returned to Knoxville, but he couldn't shake the itch for performing. He sought out other local musicians to form a group called "The Crackerjacks" and began to play at square dances and other social gatherings around town. Roy's band developed a following and they began to play on local radio shows in Knoxville under a new name, "The Crazy Tennesseans".

Two years later Roy and his band signed a recording contract with The American Records Company. After a performance, where Roy sang a hymn called *The Great Speckled Bird* an enamored executive signed the group and flew them to Chicago to record an album. When Roy and his band got to "The Windy City" they quickly learned that showbiz wasn't as glamorous as they thought. Though The Crazy Tennesseans were now professional recording artists, they had to strip down to their underwear to make it through some of the recording sessions in the smoldering hot studio that didn't have an air conditioner.

In 1938 the band came to Nashville to audition for the Opry. After bombing the first audition, Roy and his band got another try and made an impression on Opry founder George D. Hay and producer Harry Stone. Both men were blown away and invited the group to play on the hit radio show. The Crazy Tennesseans not only wowed the Opry officials, but the people listening at home too. WSM was inundated with letters from fans who wanted to hear more from Acuff and his band. Within a year The Crazy Tennesseans were renamed "The Smoky Mountain Boys" and became members of the Grand Ole Opry.

After establishing himself as a country artist, Roy Acuff started to learn the ropes as a businessman in the music industry. Around this time he had become friends with Fred Rose, a local songwriter. Rose had written hit songs for popular country artists of the time like Hank Snow, Ray Price and Hank Williams. Roy even recorded one of his tunes, *Blue Eyes Crying in the Rain* in 1945. Thirty years later Willie Nelson covered the sorrowful ballad and turned the tune into an instant country classic.

Through their friendship Roy Acuff and Fred Rose started Acuff-Rose Music. Their new venture became the first Nashville based music publishing company. Their company published over 50,000 songs including classics like Hank Williams' *I'm So Lonesome I Could Cry*, Roy Orbison's *Oh, Pretty Woman* and *I Can't Stop Loving You* that was recorded by Don Gibson and later covered by Kitty Wells, Roy Orbison, Frank Sinatra, Tina Turner,

Elvis Presley, Dolly Parton, Conway Twitty, Martina McBride, Bryan Adams and many others.

After establishing himself in entertainment and business, Roy Acuff slipped up and accidently got involved in politics in 1943. During that time, Tennessee Governor Prentice Cooper had declined an invitation to the Opry. Governor Cooper looked down his nose at country music and proclaimed that the popular radio program had made Tennessee "The Hillbilly Capital of the United States." This didn't sit too well with country music fans who wrote Roy's name in during the Republican primary and general election. The "King of Country Music" garnered only a small fraction of the vote and was soundly defeated (even though technically he wasn't actually a candidate).

Four years later, Roy answered the call of the people and went all in. The former baseball player turned entertainer officially challenged former Governor and World War II veteran Gordon Browning in the 1948 Tennessee governor's race. Running as a Republican, Roy easily won the primary with 81% of the vote. Despite juggling his duties with the Grand Ole Opry, the folksy country music star ran a legitimate campaign and was considered to be a contender due to his popularity in the state.

Basing his entire platform around the Ten Commandments from the Bible as well as "The Golden Rule", Roy Acuff vowed to treat everyone as he wished to be treated. He preached bipartisanship and promised to have a Cabinet of not only Republicans but hardworking and trustworthy Democrats as well. Roy wanted to cut taxes when possible but still increase pensions for the elderly and appropriate funds to take care of disadvantaged children, the disabled and World War II veterans. The earnest troubadour promised better schools and wanted to use the governor's office to shine a spotlight on Tennessee tourism. And to help bring in more tourism dollars, Roy insisted that he wouldn't give up any of his duties with the Opry and would still perform while he was the governor. When pressed by a reporter, Roy even doubled down on his statement and declared that he wouldn't give up performing on the radio show even if he was elected President!

Sadly, Roy's naivety was his downfall. The novice politician honestly thought he could win the race with ideas and a little help from his popularity.

Unfortunately for him, the Republicans hadn't held the Tennessee Governor's office since 1920 in a large part due to E. H. Crump. "Boss" Crump was a former United States Congressman who also served as the mayor of Memphis on two occasions. The wily politician built a blue wall around, not just Memphis, but Shelby County as well. As Crump's influence grew across the state, backdoor deals and underhanded tactics like ballot manipulation became commonplace. An honest man like Roy Acuff who turned his back on corruption and Crump's political machine didn't have a chance.

Ultimately Gordon Browning reclaimed the Governor's office winning 67% of the vote. Like always, Roy was humble in defeat. He congratulated his opponent and told reporters that he sincerely felt a better man than him was needed to run the state.

After a short-lived stint in politics, Roy Acuff returned full-time to country music after the election. However, the former politician soon found out that fiddles and Appalachian music had fallen out of favor with fans. With Elvis Presley ushering in a new era, Roy struggled to find his place in country radio competing against a new generation of artists like George Jones, Eddy Arnold, Marty Robbins and Johnny Cash.

Despite his struggle to find traction on the country charts, Roy continued to record new music and was a constant presence at the Opry. His perseverance and career was rewarded in 1962 when he became the first living person to be inducted into the Country Music Hall of Fame.

During the Vietnam War, the ever-patriotic entertainer took four trips to Vietnam during the holidays to perform for soldiers overseas. In May 1973 Roy Acuff was honored for his dedication to the armed forces in a service at the White House. While there were many entertainers on hand for the event on the White House lawn, President Richard Nixon personally asked Roy if he would perform for the dignitaries and POWs at the event. Naturally Roy said yes and tore the (White) house down with his hit song *Wabash Cannonball*. The following year Nixon returned the favor and came to the dedication ceremony of the Grand Ole Opry House.

As the years went by Acuff became a beloved legend in not just country music, but in the community as well.

Once Opryland opened in the early 1970s, Roy became a constant presence in the park as a performer and as an unofficial ambassador that greeted guests. In 1981, after the death of his beloved wife Mildred, Roy began spending even more and more time in the park. The lonely country music legend stuck around well after the park closed just to visit with the friendly staff members that the Opry legend genuinely considered to be part of his extended family.

The following year E. W. "Bud" Wendell, the President of WSM went to see with Roy at his large home across the Cumberland River overlooking the park. During the visit Bud began to sense that the 79 year old widower was lonely in the big house all by himself. Since he was so instrumental in the success of not only the Opry, but Opryland, Bud proposed building Roy a new home free of charge next door to the Grand Ole Opry House. Initially Roy resisted the offer, but after a while came around on the idea. Opryland would provide security to keep the fans at bay, but when he felt like it, the legend could venture outside and enjoy the companionship of adoring fans on his own schedule. Roy graciously accepted the offer and moved into the six gabled Colonial style house when it was completed several months later. The face of the Grand Ole Opry enjoyed his new place and was often seen laughing and holding court in front of his home with those who were visiting the theme park or Opry House.

On November 23, 1992 Roy Acuff passed away from congestive heart failure. He was 89.

Today Roy is one of only a handful of artists who sold more than 30 million records over a span of fifty years. But more importantly, he was known as being a kind-hearted man who was beloved by country music fans and those in his community.

After selling Acuff-Rose Music to Gaylord Entertainment Company in 1985 for a substantial sum, Roy shared his wealth with those in need around Nashville. While he didn't tout it publicly, Roy quietly gave a lot of his money away to those who were going through difficult times. After his death, those he had helped began talking to the media about how the singer rented hotel rooms for them when they were homeless and needed a helping hand.

The Opry star also helped many others in the area. In fact, he donated freely to area churches and colleges that needed help funding their musical departments. Roy went out of his way to buy expensive musical instruments for not just houses of worship, but local musicians who were trying to get established in Music City.

In the past few years the Roy Acuff House has been used as office space. Currently it is in the process of being converted into a museum.

Hauntings

Like many other buildings around Opryland, the Roy Acuff House is said to be haunted. Currently, the building is vacant and not available for tours. I inquired about a tour of the home but was immediately shut down by officials.

Even though no one is supposed to go in the old house while it's being turned into a museum, stories have leaked out from former security personnel who still check on the building. According to those who have been inside, footsteps have sometimes been heard going up and down the stairs at night.

Doors have also been known to open and slam shut on their own. At night the old home is said to be so creepy that more than one security guard has run out of the building after hearing or seeing something unexpected.

While it's easy to chalk the strange activity up to the ghost of Roy Acuff, those who have worked security seem to think otherwise.

"I'm pretty sure it's not Mr. Acuff," said one former Opryland security official. "There were some stories about his house when I was there, but I really think it's Lady McGavock. We saw her everywhere. She was in the park, Opry House and everywhere in between. Why wouldn't she be in the Acuff house too?"

Opryland

In the fall of 1968, as Walt Disney was looking to expand into Florida, National Life and Accident Insurance Company, the parent company for WSM merged with Third National Bank to form NLT Holdings. With over $2 billion in assets, the new corporation was one of the largest financial institutions in the country.

NLT officials saw the success Disneyland was having in Southern California and began to explore the possibilities of building a theme park in Nashville. If NLT could successfully cross-promote a theme park with WSM and the Grand Ole Opry, they could potentially make Nashville into the Hollywood of the South.

Taking the name from a popular WSM radio program, the company announced in October 1968 they were going to build a large entertainment and recreational complex called "Opryland U. S. A.". The new complex would be made up of a theme park, a new Opry House, radio and television studios and a hotel. After having worked with Disneyland and SeaWorld in California, Economic Research Associates of Los Angeles was hired to help WSM with the planning stages of Opryland.

The firm got to work right away and sent a team to Nashville to study the economic feasibility of a theme park in the area. The crew also began scouring middle Tennessee to find 150 to 200 acres away from downtown to build the new entertainment complex. Later that year Randall Duell & Associates, a Los Angeles architectural firm that had worked on Six Flags over Atlanta and Six Flags over Texas was also brought in to help develop Opryland.

On September 27, 1969 WSM's board of directors officially announced to the press that they had finalized plans to build Opryland U. S. A. The $16 million dollar entertainment and recreational complex would be centered around the Grand Ole Opry. The sprawling campus would include a new 5,000 seat Grand Ole Opry House, a theme park, an exhibit center, a country music museum, a complex of restaurants, shops and a 150 room motor lodge.

Although WSM had yet to determine Opryland's location, it was revealed that WSM had been looking at nine locations. Initially it was believed that some land along Hillsboro Road in Franklin and another piece of property in Cheatham County were the leading contenders.

A month later WSM officials threw a curveball at the media by announcing that they had acquired 369 acres in Donelson on the east side of the Cumberland River. Location was the primary factor for the decision since the property was just a short drive from the airport. At the time Briley Parkway was being expanded from Gallatin Road to Thompson Lane and WSM had received assurances from officials in local government that the road would be completed by the time the park was scheduled to open.

Officials announced the new Opryland theme park would tentatively open in the spring of 1971 and bring over 1,200 new jobs to the area. While the park would need one million visitors each year to break even, WSM brass was confident they could easily draw visitors from a 200 mile radius. With guests coming in from Atlanta, Knoxville, Memphis and Louisville, officials were confident that the new park would rival not just Disneyland, in Anaheim, California but Six Flags that had recently opened in Atlanta, Georgia.

Officials stressed that Opryland would be going for "entertainment "over "amusement" like you might find at Disneyland. Opryland General Manager Mike Downs vowed to not use animatronic characters like Disneyland did with their rides "It's a Small World", "Pirates of the Caribbean" and "Jungle Cruise". While there would be rides, the new theme park would be branded as "The Home of American Music"

On June 30, 1970 several hundred people from middle Tennessee came to a field near Pennington Bend to watch the groundbreaking ceremony for Opryland U. S. A. that was broadcast live on the air by WSM. NLT and WSM officials along with Roy Acuff and other dignitaries such as Tennessee Governor Buford Ellington and Nashville Mayor Beverly Briley were on hand to kick off the massive project.

To start the ceremony off, Grand Ole Opry legend Roy Acuff gave a speech before performing a hasty rendition of his hit song *Wabash Cannonball*. After the performance some of the dignitaries said some words and then Acuff took back over as the master of ceremonies.

Ever the traditionalist, Acuff brought the steamboat whistle that George D. Hay used to blow before every Opry performance. That afternoon in the hot summer sun, a sweaty Roy Acuff blew into the whistle and shouted Hay's infamous opening line to the Opry, "Let 'er go boys!" Two mules steered by Mayor Briley, Governor Ellington, National Life President William Weaver and WSM President Irving Waugh began to till the soil and officially break ground on Opryland U. S. A..

Once construction crews got to work on the Opryland U. S. A. campus, WSM quietly acquired 269 more acres in the area that would be used for expansion once the park was established. There was talk about tearing down the Ryman Auditorium and re-assembling it next to the park.

While the suits at WSM wanted to rebrand "The Mother Church of Country Music" into "The Little Church of Opryland", City Councilmen along with the Historical Commission wouldn't allow the structure from the 19th century to be torn down.

As Opryland U. S. A. slowly began to take shape, WSM officials held a press conference in 1971 to keep the public up to date on construction and give some details on how the theme park would be laid out. Opryland would be made up of five areas, Opry Plaza, Hill Country, New Orleans Area, American West Area and Music of Today Area.

Opry Plaza

Opry Plaza was where the main entrance into the park was located. Even if you didn't have a ticket, you had access to a lot of the Opry Plaza. People without tickets to the park could visit the gift shops and National Life

Hospitality Center that were located outside the gates to the theme park. Once you were inside the main gates, you had access to the Roy Acuff Theatre, Rudy's Farm Sausage Kitchen, a record shop, a hospitality center, several gift shops and the WSM studio where guests could watch as top disc jockeys in the country broadcast live shows from the park.

Opry Plaza was also the location of the future Grand Ole Opry House that wouldn't open until 1974.

Hill Country was designed to resemble life in an Appalachian village complete with woodworkers, glassblowers and blacksmith working at nearby shops. With the sounds of the Martha White Folk Music Show in the background, you could also hear the sound of the train rolling through a train station named "Grinder's Switch". In this area you could catch a train and ride to El Paso Train Station on the other side of the park.

While putting together the "Opryland Railroad", officials bought two antique trains, "The Vulcan" and "The Beatrice". The Vulcan was manufactured in 1920 in Wilkes Barre, Pennsylvania and originally was used to pull coal cars in the Keystone State. Upon being restored, the train was renamed "Rachel" after President Andrew Jackson's wife who lived at the nearby Hermitage in the 19th century.

The other train, the Beatrice was acquired from Georgia and had been built in 1910 by the H. K. Porter Company. It was used to transport sugar cane from St. James Plantation in Thibodaux, Louisiana.

Opryland hired former engineers that had been conductors for the L&N Railroad to carry park guests around a mile track. Chugging along at 10 miles per hour, guests could ride through the park in three shiny red, green and beige passenger cars that could each hold 80 people per trip.

The FlumeZoom
Photo Courtesy of Shawn Cook

In addition to a pottery shop and a handmade musical instrument store, Hill Country was also home to a water ride called, "The Flume Zoom". The Flume Zoom was built by the Arrow Development Company in Mountain View, California. The ride was designed to mimic the log flumes used by lumberjacks to transport logs down the river. Up to five park guests would ride in small boats made to look like hollowed out logs that traveled up an incline to a height of 40 feet. Once they reached the top of the water-filled track, the ride made its way through the treetops, before plummeting down a 30 foot plunge. Of course, the ride culminated with everyone in the boat getting soaking wet at the end of the ride.

The New Orleans Area was themed after the blues and jazz music. Buildings in this part of the park were built to replicate the architecture in the French Quarter in New Orleans, Louisiana. The highlight of this area was a show called "Everybody's Music". The 25 minute show started in the streets like a New Orleans funeral procession and made its way to the Dixieland Patio before ending in a parade. Two crews of six musicians and a female vocalist performed the show 12 to 14 times each day.

The American Music Theatre was also located in the New Orleans Area. The large amphitheater was built to host "I Hear America Singing" a 55 minute production that traced the history of music in America from the 1920s to the present day. Eighteen singers and dancers, a fourteen member orchestra and a six man technical team performed the show four times a day in two shifts.

In addition to the large musical, the New Orleans Area also featured the Ocoma Chicken Plantation restaurant, as well as several gift shops. The area was also home to the Tom Tichenor Puppet Show that took place in a painted wagon. The puppet show was performed 22 times each day by local puppeteer Tom Tichenor. Tichenor had hosted a children's show on radio for WSM and later on television for ABC.

A Skyride station was located in the New Orleans Area. The Swiss cable cars offered guests a scenic view of the park 90 feet above the ground. The ride transported up to four visitors in cable cars suspended from cables from the New Orleans Area to the Music of Today Area. The ride was built in Switzerland with safety in mind. In fact, the cars traveled with the southwestern wind currents and guests never had to worry about rocking back and forth on a windy day.

The Carousel on the Lake was also originally located in the New Orleans Area. The rolling gondola ride was built in the 1880s in Germany and purchased from an attractions company in Miami, Florida. The carousel was meticulously restored and placed in the middle of a small lake. The massive 25 ton ride was 65 feet in diameter and stood 27 feet tall. The carousel was decorated with drawings of young German girls, cherubs and bats and featured eight elaborate gondolas that resembled horse drawn carriages.

Modeled after El Paso, Texas in the 19th century, the American West Area showcased a western frontier theme. Featuring music from the west, a small theatre called "La Cantina" was home to a comedic show called, "They Went Thataway". The 20 minute show featured two crews of five singers and a piano player. Within walking distance from La Cantina you could find a blacksmith shop, a Mexican candle shop, a general store, the Chuck Wagon snack shop and a large full-service Mexican restaurant.

The Tin Lizzies
Photo Courtesy of Shawn Cook

Arguably the most popular ride in the American West area was the Tin Lizzie car ride sponsored by American

Oil. The 3 mile per hour car ride allowed a driver and up to three passengers to putt around a guided track in the backwoods of the American West Area in a replica of a Ford Model-T.

Also located in the American West Area was the Raft Ride (also known as Ryman's Ferry). Six people could board a wooden raft on Eagle Lake and leisurely float around a track that was located just underneath the water.

The Music of Today Area celebrated modern pop and rock music. The area was home to the Children's Animal Farm and the Frosty Morn Packing Company Animal Opry Show. The Animal Opry featured a dancing chicken, a guitar playing duck as well as a pig at a keyboard.

You could also find a penny arcade and numerous other shops nearby. The featured ride in the area was the Timber Topper Ride (which later became the Rock N Roller Coaster). The Timber Topper was a spiral roller coaster that rambled around in the treetops.

Another popular ride in the Music of Today Area was the Disc Jockey Ride. Similar to the teacups ride in Disneyland, up to eight people could climb inside wooden barrels that rapidly spun in a circle.

The Disc Jockey Ride

In addition to the park, a 28 acre parking lot was being built. The parking lot would hold 4,000 vehicles but could be expanded if needed. To make things easy on park guests, Opryland would offer a shuttle service that was sponsored by Third National Bank. To keep with the country music theme, each tram that went back and forth to the park was built to look like an old country bus.

Photo Courtesy of Melissa Brown

Opryland officials also announced they would be hiring 1,200 people, 450 of which would be seasonal workers that were paid $2.30 an hour. Around this time the park put out a casting call for men five feet tall and under. These staff members would be hired to wear elaborate 9′ tall costumes of stringed instrument characters. Delilah Dulcimer, Jose Mandolin, Johnny Guitar, Yancy Banjo, Frankie Fiddle and Barney Bass's jobs were to stroll through the park and greet guests as well as pose for pictures. None of the characters spoke but each had their own distinct personality.

Executives boasted that Opryland would feature 9 rides, 24 merchandise shops, 16 food outlets, 7 environmental areas and more live entertainment than any theme park in the country. In fact, Opryland U. S. A. hired Paul Crabtree, the producer/director of the Cumberland County Playhouse in Crossville to write five original musical shows. Park officials aggressively recruited dancers, musicians and singers from local colleges.

Opryland also doubled down on their promise to deliver live entertainment and worked out a deal for Opry stars to perform in the park multiple times each day of the week.

Like other theme parks in the country, Opryland would be open on weekends in May through Memorial Day. After Memorial Day, the theme park would be open every day through the summer until Labor Day.

While Opryland needed to draw one million visitors to break even, WSM predicted 1.2 million guests would visit the theme park during the first year, 800,000 of which would come from out of state.

On June 23 1971, Opryland U. S. A. took one step closer to becoming a reality when a visitor's center was opened on the property. 250 spectators along with some of the executives from National Life and Accident Insurance Company gathered near where the Opry Plaza was being built for a modest grand opening ceremony. Tennessee Governor Winfield Dunn had the honor of cutting a ceremonial red, white and blue ribbon to officially open the facility.

Four local women were hired to be hostesses for the new visitor's center. The facility featured a 33 square foot model of Opryland U. S. A. that the hostesses used to show potential future guests how the park would be laid out.

The visitor's center quickly became a busy place as locals began to pop in and out to get the latest news and info on the park. However, three months later the center shut down so the Opryland model could be taken on the road. Opryland officials had worked out deals with shopping centers in Alabama, Kentucky and other parts of Tennessee for the model to be set up so they could drum up interest in the new theme park in Nashville.

Opryland also hired 21 permanent security guards called "Rangers". In addition to the rangers that patrolled the complex, 34 more seasonal employees were hired to patrol the park by foot, horseback, golf cart and by boat on the Cumberland River.

A First Aid Station was also opened in the complex. The building was equipped with seven beds and everything medical personnel might need to help guests who had become dehydrated or any other ailment they might sustain while spending the day at the park. To staff the First Aid Station, Opryland officials hired a registered nurse as well as two aides.

Hiccups

In early 1972 excitement began to build in the community for Opryland U. S. A. However, internally lots of things were starting to go wrong. One night after dark, a night watchman noticed someone wearing black clothing coming out of one of the buildings that was under construction. When the patrolman ordered him to stop, the intruder fired a gun at the security guard. After a brief firefight the gunman fled under the dark of night. Even though Opryland put out a $5,000 reward for information leading to the intruder's arrest, no one was ever arrested.

A few months' later three local millwrights who had a dispute with their union began picketing in front of the park and blocked traffic on Briley Parkway. After ignoring commands from a park security guard, Michael Downs the General Manager of the park made a citizen's arrest and took all three men to a nearby police station. The millwrights were given fines and received suspended sentences.

On April 28th more unhappy union members from the Teamsters, Chauffeurs, Helpers & Taxicab Drivers from Local Union No 327 set up approximately 30 pickets around the park. Protesting the fact that Opryland trucks were being driven by employees instead of teamsters, the group started causing problems. The group blocked cars from coming and going and threatened employees who were coming in to prepare for the park's Grand Opening.

Things got so hectic that Metro Chancellor Ned Lentz got involved. Hoping to keep the peace, the respected judge issued a restraining order against the Union. The order worked for a day or two but within a few days the Teamsters, Chauffeurs, Helpers & Taxicab Drivers were joined by over 200 men from the Operating Engineers Union on the picket lines. Once again, Chancellor Lentz stepped in and handed down another injunction. This order allowed the teamsters to picket but limited the union to two men for each entrance.

After a few days the matter was resolved. Things went back to normal at Opryland and the crew worked around the clock to put the finishing touches on the new theme park. Unfortunately, in the early morning hours of May 6th, forty construction workers that were unhappy about non-union employees being brought in to wrap up construction began picketing at an entrance to the park. The picketers were loud and very vocal that morning but as the day went on they began to get violent. The disgruntled union members didn't just hurl insults; they started throwing rocks that smashed a handful of car windshields.

As word got around about the busted car windshields, rumors began circulating that an even larger demonstration was going to start later in the day. Already feeling uneasy due to the tension from the unions in the previous days, Opryland General Manager Mike Downs made the call and sent over 800 employees home early.

Fortunately Opryland and the teamsters reached a deal and crews got back to work. Due to all the hiccups the Grand Opening got pushed back from May 6th to May 27th.

The rescheduled Grand Opening didn't sit too well with eager locals who wanted to see the new theme park. Late one afternoon in mid-May, a handful of rambunctious teenagers swam across the Cumberland River to get a sneak peek of the park. As the kids walked around and took it all in, they were greeted by park rangers who apprehended them and threw them out.

Grand Opening

On Saturday, May 27th Opryland U. S. A. officially opened three weeks after it was originally scheduled. Thousands of people from middle Tennessee and the surrounding areas packed the new theme park to check things out.

Admission was fairly inexpensive during the inaugural season. Tickets cost $5.25 for adults and $3.50 for kids under 12. Children 5 and under got in for free. Season passes which offered unlimited visits to the park were also available for $16.

There were no age restrictions on rides but some attractions had height restrictions for safety reasons. For instance, in order to ride the Timber Topper you had to be at least 48 inches tall so the safety bar system could hold you safely in place during the ride. Those that weren't tall enough could easily slip out under the bar and fall out of the ride.

To celebrate the opening weekend, WSMV, Channel 4 in Nashville, (Who was also owned by NLT) aired an hour long special called "Opryland U. S. A". The event was hosted by "Tennessee" Ernie Ford and Johnny Cash. The show featured Marty Robbins, Roy Acuff, Minnie Pearl and several other prominent country and western stars performing some of their hit songs around the new theme park.

After the opening weekend, Opryland showed no signs of slowing down as guests continued to visit the park. Businesses took note and began working with Opryland U. S. A. to capitalize on the theme park's success. Coca-Cola offered a coupon for $1.25 off of lunch in the park in exchange for twelve bottle caps. Frosty Morn, the sponsor of the Animal Opry, began offering a free child's admission in exchange for ten labels from a package of their sausage or hot dogs. One ambitious local car dealer even began offering free family passes to the park with the purchase of a new automobile.

Opryland officials estimated they would have 1.2 million guests from Memorial Day to Labor Day in 1972. In those first 108 days, the park exceeded expectations and brought in over 1.4 million people.

Due to the success in their first year, Opryland added a new restaurant, more restrooms, a new country music themed show and 800 more parking spaces for the 1973 season.

Opryland's second season was also a hit. In fact, attendance was up 22% with 1.7 million guests visiting the park in 1973. As exciting as the turnout was, Opryland officials were even more optimistic about 1974. With the Grand Opening of the new Grand Ole Opry House, Opryland's third season would surely be bigger than the second. Of course, their projections were correct. In 1974 over 1.8 million guests visited the park.

The Flood of 1975

With attendance increasing every year, executives were already giddy about the upcoming 1975 season. However, Mother Nature had different ideas. On March 12th and 13th 1975, a massive storm front moved through Nashville that dumped six inches of rain on Music City. By the 13th the already swollen Cumberland River had risen six feet above flood levels and turned the theme park into a muddy lake. The Grand Ole Opry was moved to the Municipal Auditorium and Opryland officials got to work assessing the damage.

As soon as it was safe, crews got to work cleaning up the swampy theme park. Crews worked diligently around the clock to put Opryland back together.

In late March 1975, Opryland held a tent sale to get rid of all of the damaged merchandise left over in the gift shops from the previous seasons. Over 6,000 people came to the event to get deals on records, film, records and other items that may have had a little dried mud on them from the flood.

Even though Opryland had to push their opening date back two weeks, over 10,000 people packed the park on April 19th when Opryland officially opened for the 1975 season. That year the park rolled out a new area called "The State Fair "on some land that had been included in the American West Area in the northwest corner of Opryland.

The State Fair Area included several new rides for guests to enjoy like the Country Bumpkin Bumper Cars and Tennessee Waltz swings.

Tennessee Waltz Swings
Photo Courtesy of Shawn Cook

The biggest hit of the new area was the Wabash Cannonball roller coaster. Taking its name from the hit Roy Acuff song about a steam locomotive, the Wabash Cannonball zipped and dipped over 1,200 feet of track before dashing upside down through two 73 foot high corkscrews at 45 miles an hour.

The Wabash Cannonball

Adding a second large roller coaster proved to be a hit and Opryland attendance increased by over 100,000 people from 1974 despite opening two weeks late.

Momentum

In 1976 and 1977 Opryland kept the momentum going by drawing over 2 million visitors for the first time each year.

Seeing exponential growth year after year, the park began tinkering and experimenting with the Music of Today Area in 1977. Opryland officials saw that guests were responding to 1950s-style music over contemporary tunes and opted to revamp rides and restaurants and renamed the area "Do Wah Diddy City" for the 1978 season. Staff members that worked in Chubby's Drive In, Papa Varallo's Chili and Pizza Parlor and the Great Balls of Fire Arcade wore poodle skirts, bobby socks, saddle oxfords and in some cases, roller skates.

The Disc Jockey ride that originally spun visitors around in wooden barrels outside was converted into the Little Deuce Coupe ride. The teacup-style ride was updated and moved indoors into a geodesic dome. The Timber Topper roller coaster also received a new coat of paint and was rechristened as "The Rock N Roller Coaster".

The Jukebox Theater
Photo Courtesy of Shawn Cook

To celebrate the new themed area Dick Clark, from the hit TV show "American Bandstand" was brought in for two days to host shows in the brand new Juke Box Theater. Notable bands from the 1950s such as The Shirelles, Bo Diddley and Freddie Cannon Clark appeared to help celebrate the opening of Do Wah Diddy City

The Barnstormer
Photo Courtesy of Shawn Cook

While all the new bells and whistles in Do Wah Diddy City were pretty popular, the most exciting new feature in 1978 was a ride called "The Barnstormer" in the new Lakeside Area. The Barnstormer ride featured twelve vintage Waldo Pepper bi-planes that could hold up to four park guests. The planes were slowly raised to the top of a 92 foot tall tower by hydraulics. Passengers had a bird's eye view of the park as the planes spun around in a circle before dropping 40 feet back to the landing in the middle of Eagle Lake. The Barnstormer was a very popular ride. However, there was often grumbling from park guests because it was often closed. Anytime there were strong winds, the ride was not safe to ride and had to be closed from time to time.

A new concert venue also opened up in 1979. The Roy Acuff Theater named in honor of the Opry legend was located next door to the Grand Ole Opry House. The theater was usually used for some of the larger named performers that performed in the park like "Little" Jimmy Dickens and Porter Wagoner. Naturally, Roy Acuff would stop by from time to time to join his friends on stage or perform a set when he had some free time.

With a revamped Do Wah Diddy City, the new Barnstormer ride and the Roy Acuff Theater, you would think Opryland officials would be content with their 1979 lineup, right? Nope. The park also announced two Soap Opera festivals that summer that featured meet and greets with stars from the popular daytime shows like "All My Children" and "The Young and the Restless". Opryland also tried to piggy-back off the popularity of Star Wars by announcing a state of the art computer programmed laser show featuring choreographed laser beams, lights and sound effects that synced up with popular modern day Top 40 hits.

With so many new features in 1979, you would think that Opryland brought in over 2 million guests for the third year in a row. Unfortunately a nationwide gas shortage crippled tourism in Nashville. While other parks and attractions were down over 25% in the country, Opryland was only down 9% and still brought in 1.9 million visitors.

In 1980 Opryland signed a deal with Marvel comics that allowed them to use popular characters like Spider-Man, The Incredible Hulk, Green Goblin, The Thing and other Marvel superheroes that summer. The comic book stars greeted children and signed autographs in designated areas in the park.

While meeting a superhero was thrilling to kids, adults had the opportunity to meet Larry Hagman in the park in August. Hagman starred as the always-scheming J. R. Ewing on the hit primetime soap opera "Dallas". The show left viewers in suspense that March when Hagman's character, J. R. Ewing was shot by an unknown gunman (or gunwoman) in the season finale. Hagman ducked and dodged questions from fans that desperately wanted spoilers about their favorite show during his weekend of meet and greets at the park.

1980 proved to be a banner year for the theme park with over 2.1 million visitors making their way through Opryland's turnstiles. Opryland executives were cautiously optimistic that they would break 2.2 million guests, but a very wet spring and an extended heat wave in July kept some guests at home.

After seeing success from adding new attractions in 1979, Opryland went all in 1981 and added a new area in the northern part of the park called "Grizzly Country". The feature attraction in Grizzly Country was the Grizzly River Rampage. The Grizzly River Rampage was a white water rafting adventure ride that took up ten acres.

Photo Courtesy of Tiffany Sanchez

The ride started with a large black conveyor belt bringing a large 12 person raft to the landing. After boarding, guests calmly floated down the Grizzly River with peaceful music playing in the background. As people rode down the river occasionally they might get stuck on a waterfall, which of course soaked just about everyone onboard. Suddenly, things started to get a little chaotic and the music became more frantic. The white water rapids forcefully push the raft downstream and into a dark cave. And just when there is a light at the end of the tunnel a huge grizzly bear emerges from a dark corner and lets out a ferocious growl.

The Grizzly River Rampage
Photo Courtesy of Shawn Cook

To kick off the Grand Opening festivities for Grizzly Country, actor Dan Haggerty from the hit TV show "Grizzly Adams" was brought in to sign autographs and take pictures. Park officials also put together a group of musicians who played in various shows and had them perform a few shows during the opening weekend. "The Grizzly River Boys" became quite popular and became a full-time act in the park. The group changed their name to "The Tennessee River Boys" and again to what they are known as today, "Diamond Rio". Perhaps you've heard of them?

Opryland also made a deal with General Mills and brought in the Breakfast Buddies to greet park guests. Children got to take pictures with Franken Berry, Honey Nut Bee, Count Chocula and Trix Rabbit in various parts of the park that summer.

In addition to the Grizzly River Ride and the characters on the front of the cereal boxes, Opryland also announced a 1982 concert series. Established performers Conway Twitty, Reba McEntire, Ricky Skaggs, George Strait and Tammy Wynette and several others were brought in to entice a different crowd that might not be intrigued by the big scary Grizzly bear.

Due to the success of the terrifying new white water rafting ride, Opryland drew its largest crowd ever in 1981. A record 2.2 million visitors came to the theme park that summer. According to park officials, 1.2 million of those guests rode the Grizzly River Rampage.

Changes

In 1982 Opryland held steady with another 2.2 million guests. But change was in the air in the fall of that year when American General bought NLT.

Shortly thereafter, American General sent shockwaves through Nashville when they announced they were going to sell off some of their non-insurance assets like Opryland and the Opryland Hotel. Six potential buyers emerged from the dust, Marriott, Anheuser Busch, U. S. Tobacco Company, Shoneys, Kroger and a local businessman E. Bronson Ingram.

Ingram along with former NLT chairman Walter Robinson and National Life President C. A. Craig II put together an offer for $275 million to buy Opryland USA, Opryland Hotel, The Grand Ole Opry, the AM and FM radio stations and The Nashville Network. After some negotiations, things fell apart and American General rejected their offer.

After American General expressed interest in selling Opryland to a local group, a small group of local investors began talking with the large insurance company. The investors were successful in getting several Grand Ole Opry stars like John Conlee and Jerry Clower to buy in as minority owners, but ultimately negotiations with American General never got that far.

Even though ownership was up in the air, Opryland opened in the spring of 1983 like it always did. There were no new rides but there were special concerts with legendary performers like Wayne Newton and Chet Atkins.

On July 1, 1983, in the middle of the season, a press conference was held on the stage of the Grand Ole Opry. That afternoon it was announced that the Gaylord Broadcasting Company had purchased American General's Opryland assets for $250 million. Though it had been announced that American wanted to sell to a local group, Gaylord Broadcasting from Dallas wound up being the top bidder. Gaylord was loosely affiliated with WSM as the producer of the hit TV show "Hee Haw", but the company made most of their money from their TV and radio stations in New Orleans, Tampa, Dallas, Cleveland, Seattle and other major markets around the country.

Within a few months Gaylord took out full page ads in local newspapers touting how they were the perfect fit for the Opryland properties. The new owners also vowed to not change anything about the theme park or Grand Ole Opry.

At the end of the 1983 Opryland season, the theme park finished the year 10% down from the previous year. While drawing a very respectable 2.0 million guests, the park was hampered by Conway Twitty's new venture, "Twitty City". The *Hello Darlin'* crooner opened a smaller country music entertainment complex in nearby Hendersonville, Tennessee. Gaylord officials also chalked up some of the downturn in guests to the grand opening of Epcot in Walt Disney World in Orlando, Florida.

The Gaylord Era

The Screamin' Delta Demon

In 1984 Gaylord began to make a few changes to Opryland. The Screamin' Delta Demon roller coaster was added to the New Orleans Area in the southwest corner of the theme park. Up to six passengers boarded a Bobsled that was painted up like an alligator. Once the Bobsled left the gate, riders ripped through bayou country and the delta swamp over a swampy tree-filled ravine at 40 miles per hour.

Due to the excitement surrounding the ride, Gaylord opted to build a new park entrance in the New Orleans Area so guests could jump right in line for the new attraction.

Gaylord also increased the ticket price to $13.25. If guests wanted to purchase two day tickets those were also available for $18.00.

That summer the park held steady with 2.0 million guests. It's likely there would've been a slight uptick but the park had to close for two days in May when heavy rains caused some minor flooding.

In 1985 there were no major changes to the park except you could purchase a "tricket". The tricket allowed you to visit the park for three consecutive days for the low price of $13.95. Season passes were available for $39.95.

Just outside the park, a 300 foot Victorian showboat called "The General Jackson" offered sightseeing dinner and entertainment cruises on the Cumberland River. A separate ticket was needed for the General Jackson and was not included in the price of admission to the theme park.

Due to the popularity of the Grizzly River Rampage, the Screamin' Delta Demon and the tricket, it was a banner year for Opryland U. S. A. A record-shattering 2.4 million people visited the park in 1985.

To celebrate Opryland's 15th birthday the park rolled out the red carpet in 1986. On opening day, a golf cart was also converted into a cakemobile that drove around the park. Staff members happily passed out slices of birthday cake to visitors to celebrate 15 wonderful years.

That afternoon 15,000 helium-filled balloons were released into the air by park personnel and guests. Whoever found the one that traveled the farthest distance would receive an Opryland mini-vacation. Although there was a lot of excitement for their 15th birthday, the park had a big surprise in store for their 30 millionth visitor. On August 15, 1986 an unsuspecting visitor from Hermann, Missouri was shocked when she was asked to step away from the park gates and awarded the grand prize. Opryland officials handed her two American Airline tickets and vouchers for a rental car and coupons for a year's supply of Coca-Cola.

With no new attractions, attendance dipped slightly in 1986 to 2.3 million. Opryland officials blamed the downturn on a lot of rain in June and unbearable heat in July and August.

For the 1987 season Opryland raised ticket prices and did away with the tricket. For the low price of $15.95 a general admission ticket was now good for three consecutive days to the park.

Opryland also did away with the Raft Ride and brought in a new attraction called "The Old Mill Scream". Guests walked through a cave in a mountain before boarding a large 20 passenger boat. Once the ride began, guests were pulled up the mountain before making a 180 degree turn and plunging 50 feet into Eagle Lake at 44 miles per hour. Though the ride was rather short, park visitors were all but guaranteed to get wet and a chance to cool off on a hot summer day.

The Old Mill Scream

After disembarking the Old Mill Scream, the former passengers exited through an old grist mill, then through a walkway that was located directly in front of where the boats splashdown in spectacular fashion. Those that weren't paying attention would get wet again when a boat splashed into Eagle Lake right in front of them! Typically the walkway was packed with kids that weren't tall enough to ride. Even though they couldn't ride, if they waited a few minutes, they were all but assured of getting splashed.

The Old Mill Scream
Photo Courtesy of Shawn Cook

The Old Mill Scream was a hit and park attendance hit record levels by once again drawing in over 2.4 million in 1987.

In advance of the upcoming season Opryland officials were aggressive in promoting what was coming up in the spring of 1988. Although the park quietly raised ticket prices by two dollars, Opryland offered season tickets at a discounted rate of $35 if you bought them before the end of the year. Naturally, in December they advertised how season passes made wonderful Christmas gifts in the local newspapers.

Officials also wanted to freshen up the entertainment in the park for the 1988 season. Country legend Brenda Lee was brought in for a residency and was the star of an elaborate 75 minute stage show called, "Music, Music, Music". Lee performed the show twice a day during the weekends in the spring and fall and twice a day, six times a week during the summer. While Lee sang all of her hits like *I'm Sorry*, she also performed other classic songs like Judy Garland's *Over the Rainbow* and Elvis Presley's *I Can't Help Falling in Love with You*.

Opryland also featured several contests in 1988. The grand prize was a free trip to the CMA Awards. Smaller prizes like cameras and tickets to concerts were also available.

Attendance fell to 2.2 million visitors in 1988. While Gaylord and Opryland officials blamed the drop on economic conditions, everyone knew it was because people wanted a fresh, new ride each year to keep them interested.

In 1989 Opryland opened an indoor roller coaster called "Chaos" that spring next to the Grizzly River Rampage. The new ride was considered to be one of the most innovative roller coasters in the country and cost $7 million to build. The attraction was so advanced for its time; it was produced by two different companies. Netherlands ride manufacturer Vckoma International and Hollywood video effects gurus R/Greenburg Associates worked together to produce a state of the art attraction that combined a roller coaster with modern audio-visual technology.

Before the ride started, passengers boarded a 240 foot train with 40 cars that held two people. Once the ride started the passengers were hurled through the dark inside a 2.1 million cubic foot building while strange images like a clock, fire or other things were displayed above and below the riders by a projector.

Chaos
Photo Courtesy of Shawn Cook

When working properly, roughly 1,500 people could ride each hour. Unfortunately, Opryland had a hard time getting the kinks worked out of the ride as it spent a lot of time out of order after it opened.

Even with the problems, Chaos was insanely popular with park guests. Opryland went all out with their advertising and put the new ride's logo on 35 million Coca-Cola cans as well as 3.5 million Purity milk cartons in middle Tennessee. In late March when the ride officially opened, actor Corey Feldman was brought in to meet fans and sign autographs.

All of Opryland's hard work paid off because Chaos had almost a million riders in its inaugural season. In fact, park guests sometimes waited up to two hours just to ride the new indoor roller coaster.

To help pay for the expensive new attraction Opryland increased ticket prices by one dollar bringing the cost of a general admission ticket $18.95.

That year Opryland hit over 2.4 million visitors once again and set a single day record with 41,492 visitors on August 12. Yet, the 2.4 million number was slightly skewed. In 1989 the theme park hosted its first ever Halloween festival and stayed open on the weekend through October instead of shutting down after Labor Day.

After spending $7 million on Chaos, Opryland opted to focus on entertainment instead of a new ride for the 1990 season. The Jukebox Theater was removed and a much larger venue called the "Chevrolet Geo Theater" was built in its place in Doo Wah Diddy City. A special concert series called "Heart of Country" that featured popular artists like Lee Greenwood, Louise Mandrell,

Marie Osmond, Tammy Wynette and Gary Morris was scheduled during the summer.

That season attendance at the theme park dropped to 2.1 million. Gaylord and Opryland officials blamed the dip on competition in Branson, Missouri where older established country stars like Mel Tillis and Mickey Gilley opened their own theaters. However, everyone who lived in the area knew it was because they raised ticket prices by a dollar and didn't add any new rides.

The 1991 season saw the park sign Louise Mandrell to a deal that would lock her into a residency for most of the year. The new show was called "Love My Country" and featured Mandrell singing, dancing and playing a variety of instruments. The show was themed as a tribute to the United States military that was fighting overseas in the Gulf War, while also honoring country music.

The show featured a fourteen piece band along with nine dancers and was performed twice each day in the Acuff Theater.

In addition to the Louise Mandrell residency, Opryland also announced a 92 show concert series featuring stars like Ricky Skaggs, Vince Gill, Charlie Daniels, Travis Tritt and other popular country music performers.

Although Opryland raised ticket prices by two dollars to $21.95, attendance actually increased slightly for the 1991 season. That season 2.2 million guests visited the park.

In 1992 Opryland opted to raise ticket prices again, this time by one dollar. Season passes were available for $44.95 until the park opened. At that point the cost increased by $5.

Without a new ride, park officials doubled down on music and entertainment and brought in country music legend Porter Wagoner to be an ambassador for the park. At that stage of his career Wagoner had decided to stop touring and only play the Grand Ole Opry on the weekends. Since he was already playing the Opry and lived nearby, a deal was struck for the legendary performer to greet fans in the park on Friday, Saturday and Sundays.

After experimenting with live concerts the previous seasons, Opryland added even more shows with notable acts like Vince Gill, Restless Heart, Crystal Gayle and Lori Morgan. Unfortunately, unlike the concert series in 1991, park guests had to shell out an additional $5 to attend the shows.

Despite an emphasis on live music, attendance dropped again in 1992 to 2 million. While Opryland officials were disappointed, it was apparently obvious that without a new attraction people quickly lost interest in the theme park.

In 1993 Opryland left ticket prices alone but still charged an additional fee for the concert series that was held at the Chevrolet Geo Theater in Doo Wah Diddy City. Instead of charging $5 for the special shows, Opryland raised those prices by fifty cents to see stars like Doug

Stone, Tanya Tucker, Joe Diffie, Tracy Lawrence and Conway Twitty.

That season, even without a new ride, Opryland visitors jumped to 2.2 million. But, they also kept the park open an additional six weeks through December to coincide with the Opryland Hotel's "Country Christmas. By adding Christmas-themed shows and offering discounted $10 tickets for adults and $6 tickets for children, Opryland was able to inflate their numbers for the Gaylord shareholders.

After losing over $8 million on their concert series at the Chevrolet Geo Theater in 1993, Opryland began charging $12.95 to $19.95 to see performances by acts like Alabama, Oak Ridge Boys, George Jones, Tammy Wynette, Little Texas and Patty Loveless in 1994. However, if you bought a general admission ticket to the park, the price to see the show was reduced to $5.

Beginning of the End

While Opryland's attendance held flat at 2.2 million in 1994, rumors were going around that Gaylord was unhappy with the theme park's numbers and had put it up for sale. Officials from Turner Broadcasting as well as Disney supposedly began sniffing around Nashville to see what the asking price was.

Even though rumors were swirling about the future of Opryland, Gaylord opened their wallet and wrote a check for $8.5 million for a new rollercoaster called "The Hangman" in the American West Area. The Hangman was an inverted roller coaster that resembled a ski lift where passengers sat down as their feet dangled in the air. The ride started out by lifting riders 115 feet into the air before plunging 108 feet at 60 miles an hour. But the fun wasn't over; passengers had to endure a 360 degree heartline loop followed by several twists and turns before the ride came to an end.

 The new inverted roller coaster came with a cost that impacted those who grew up going to the park on a regular basis. The Tin Lizzie ride was removed and the replica Model-Ts were sold to Kentucky Kingdom in Louisville, Kentucky. Looking back, thanks to the Tin Lizzie ride at Opryland, I can honestly say that the Ford Motel-T was the first car I ever drove.

In addition to adding The Hangman, Opryland also added the Skycoaster in the State Fair Area. The new suspended swinging attraction gave guests the experience of jumping out an airplane and bungee jumping at the same time.

Those who were brave enough to ride the Skycoaster were raised to the top of a launch tower roughly 100 feet in the air. Once the ripcord was pulled, guests would free-fall 50 feet then would be sent soaring another 100 feet at 60 miles an hour. Naturally, gravity would pull the riders back again, back and forth like a pendulum until the Skycoaster operators slowly lowered them to the ground safely.

Unlike any other ride in the park, the Skycoaster wasn't included in the price of general admission. Guests that wanted to ride the Skycoaster had to dish out an additional $24.95 to ride the attraction. However, there were price breaks if you wanted to ride with one or two friends.

Opryland also brought back more special concerts in 1995. The Evening Concert Series featured stars like Willie Nelson, Johnny Cash, Faith Hill and Billy Ray Cyrus. Tickets ranged from $14.95 to $26.95 in addition to the regular price of admission which had increased to $28.99.

Even with a new ride, attendance dropped in 1995 at Opryland. With 2.1 million visitors, the park was still very profitable. However, the dip in the numbers was concerning, especially with the increasing competition from Dollywood in East Tennessee. In just a few years the Pigeon Forge, Tennessee-based theme park had already eclipsed 2 million visitors and was perceived a legitimate threat to Opryland U. S. A. Even more troubling for Opryland was the fact that Dollywood was drawing the same number of visitors with fewer attractions and tickets that were three dollars cheaper.

When you compared Opryland with Six Flags Over Georgia, the Atlanta-based park had added nine large rides in the last 13 years. In that time span, Opryland only added five. Instead of investing in large attractions to bring in more park guests, Gaylord opted to add a new show or two. While Opryland would make occasional tweaks to existing rides, the industry standard was to add a new one every other year.

Stop The Bleeding

After a disappointing 1995 season Gaylord entered into negotiations with Six Flags to take over park operations in 1996. Yet, despite the talks, a deal was never reached and Opryland began to plan for business as usual for the upcoming season. Naturally, after spending several million dollars for The Hangman, Opryland officials opted to not add any new attractions. Instead, the theme park once again went back to promoting popular country music acts as the main selling point for Opryland U. S. A. However, after losing millions of dollars on the shows in the previous three seasons, Opryland scaled back the concert series to only 50 dates. The park hoped to appeal to a younger crowd with newer stars like Billy Ray Cyrus, Martina McBride and Bryan White, but also sprinkled in a few legendary performers like Willie Nelson, Merle Haggard and Barbara Mandrell to appeal to older fans too.

But Opryland officials knew they had to do something else to set them apart from competitors like Dollywood and Six Flags Over Georgia. Thinking outside of the box, they decided to host a daily game show inside the park each day. Each day 42 visitors to the park were chosen at random to participate in "The $25,000 Game Show". Former "Newlyweds" game show host Bob Eubanks was brought in to host the show. While park guests had a chance to win the grand prize of $25,000 or a new car, typically they went home with a few hundred dollars or a small prize like a CD player.

Despite the emphasis on live country music and a new game show, 1996 was a failure. Park attendance dropped 9% to 1.9 million. Opryland officials tried to spin it and put the blame on Dollywood and the appeal of the theaters and outlet malls in the Smoky Mountains. In addition to Dollywood who had drawn 2.1 million guests that year, Opryland brass also tried to put some of the blame on the rise of casinos in Tunica, Mississippi. Like Dollywood, new casinos located just outside of Memphis were believed to be syphoning off visitors from Opryland.

In an effort to stop the bleeding, Opryland didn't raise ticket prices for the 1997 season but they had begun charging $5 to park. Season passes did go up $20 to $79.99 but they also included free parking with the pass.

Once again Opryland officials opted to not add any new rides but did revamp two existing attractions. The children's teacup ride was remodeled and rebranded as "Tykes Tugs". By enlarging the teacups, parents could ride with their children. Over in the State Fair Area the bumper cars area was also enlarged. This change allowed more people to ride in the cars at one time therefore decreasing the wait times in line.

 The other change in the State Fair Area was the removal of The Skycoaster. It was completely disassembled and moved to Eagle Lake where it would have greater visibility (and make more money).

The End

That summer as Opryland sputtered along trying to remain relevant, Gaylord CEO Bud Wendell retired and a war for the park's future began to take place behind closed doors. Wendell's successor, Terry E. London began looking at ways to reinvent Opryland but was leery of investing a lot of money into the 26 year old theme park.

Gaylord executives got to work and began visiting casinos in Las Vegas, Nevada and Downtown Disney in Orlando, Florida. If they could figure out a formula for combining hotels, rides, restaurants and shops, maybe they could revive Opryland U. S. A. to the glory it once had in the 1980s.

While there were factions at Gaylord that wanted to save Opryland, there were some executives who had looked at doing something completely different. A large shopping center had been discussed internally as far back as 1988. As the park began to struggle, Gaylord started looking at a massive overhaul of the Opryland U. S. A. campus. In addition to the theme park, hotel and Opry House, a sprawling complex that contained a mall, restaurants, a theater and a television studio for TNN was considered but ultimately never greenlit.

In September 1997 Gaylord announced there would be some changes to Opryland in 1998. According to the executives, major retail concepts would be incorporated inside the theme park. After word leaked to the press about Gaylord executives meeting with local politicians to talk about their ideas, rumors quickly began to spread. Would Gaylord turn Opryland into a Mall of America-type complex that combined a theme park with a large retail shopping center? Bass Pro Shops, a company that Gaylord owned a majority share in was linked to the project. The outdoor superstore had broken ground across Briley Parkway but had halted construction in order to reevaluate their options.

The following month Gaylord sold TNN and CMT to Westinghouse Electric for $1.55 billion. By selling off two profitable assets, the company was forced to restructure and many began to wonder what that meant for the theme park.

On November 4, 1997 the axe finally fell. Gaylord held a press event with the media and local leaders to announce that Opryland U. S. A. would be closing on December 31st. In its place they would build a 1.2 million square foot mall with 200 specialty shops, restaurants, a movie theater, small rides and an arcade that would employ 5,000 people. The new "Shoppertainment" complex was tentatively scheduled to open sometime in 2000.

While the park drew 1.9 million visitors in its final season, attendance was down 13% from 1994. Despite the decline in ticket sales and revenue, Opryland was still profitable. But from a business point of view Gaylord saw that park guests were spending just over $26 at Opryland the past few seasons. Yet, with a new mall on the property, it was believed that customers would spend $26 in their first few fifteen minutes shopping. And best of all, the mall wasn't a seasonal business with expensive rides that constantly needed maintenance. The mall would be open year 'round and as a landlord they could collect rent 12 months out of the year.

Gaylord partnered with Mills Corp to build the new mall. Mills Corp had developed other large size shopping centers around the country. Their most recent mall in Fort Lauderdale, Florida had been drawing 20 million people per year. By partnering with Mills Corp, Gaylord got to share the costs of building the new mall and also got to work with an established company with a background in "Shoppertainment". But the new partnership wouldn't come cheap. Gaylord gave up 2/3 ownership of the new mall to Mills Corp but maintained 1/3 share of the new venture.

The new mall was universally panned by just about everyone outside of Gaylord, Mills Corp and a few politicians that had been involved in the process. While Gaylord promised 5,000 new jobs in 2000, they had effectively done away with 275 full time jobs and 1,700 seasonal jobs. Opryland was beloved by locals who took their children to the park each year. Even in 2021, Opryland's closing is still a sore subject among many in Nashville.

As all of this was playing out in Nashville, Opryland was still in business and had visitors in the theme park. On November 15th, Opryland had a 50% off liquidation sale in the parking lot for all remaining park gift shop souvenir merchandise like shirts, hats, glassware, toys and other items. Opryland held another liquidation event in December that also included park signs. At the end of the sale, whatever merchandise was left over was eventually donated to the Salvation Army.

On December 31st, 1997 Opryland closed their gates for good.

After the park was shut down, rides were disassembled and sold to the highest bidder. The Old Indiana Fun Park bought The Hangman, Wabash Cannonball, The Dulcimer Splash, Little Deuce Coupe, the Rock N Roller Coaster as well as the two Opryland trains. The Skycoaster, which was leased, went back to its owner and eventually rented out to another park.

Opryland Attendance

When you look at a graph, it's easy to see how the attendance would rise and fall based on new rides like The Grizzly River Rampage and The Hangman. Once Opryland started touting concerts or new musicals, it was easy to see that Gaylord didn't want to spend the money to keep up with other theme parks around the country. In the last few years in operation, the plan to bring in well-known country artists blew up in Opryland's face when the performers got a large pay day that ultimately didn't translate into increased ticket sales. From 1994 to 1997 Opryland lost over $10 million from their concert series. Had Gaylord allocated those funds differently and built one, or possibly two new large rides, it is possible Opryland would still be in business.

Below is a chart that breaks down Opryland's attendance by the millions per year. You can see that a decrease in the final years, visitors were still coming to the park in droves.

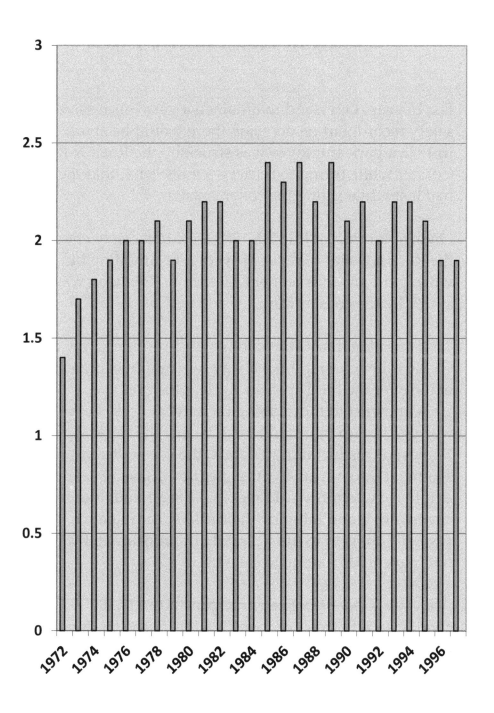

Death at the Theme Park

For 26 years Opryland maintained a very impressive safety record, but on occasion there would be an accident. In 1978 a park employee was struck by the Rock N Roller Coaster while trying to retrieve a guest's hat that they had lost while riding the roller coaster.

On the morning of July 30, 1980 a routine safety check on the Rock n Roller Coaster proved to be anything but safe when park groundskeeper Clarence E. Robinson was struck by the coaster train.

That morning, park staff conducted a routine safety check on the roller coaster. Like always an announcement was made over the loud speaker to clear the area. Unbeknownst to those doing the safety check, Robinson was picking up limbs and trash beside the track. As Robinson was picking up debris, the coaster train slammed into him at 45 miles per hour. The 59 year old employee was thrown 15 feet into the air and later found covered in blood lying by the track. An ambulance rushed Robinson to the hospital but unfortunately nothing could be done to save him.

After the accident police and Opryland officials conducted an extensive investigation. Some speculated that Robison may have tried to commit suicide while others believed that he simply had bad hearing and didn't hear the announcement to clear the track. Ultimately the family sued Opryland's parent company

NLT as well as the Arrow Development Company who built the ride. A large check was written and the matter quietly went away.

Sadly Clarence Robinson wouldn't be the only person that died in the theme park. On June 17, 1984 an eight year old boy from Knoxville collapsed while riding the Wabash Cannonball. Once the ride stopped, he was found unconscious. Medical personnel tried to revive the boy but were unsuccessful. Though the child's death happened on the Wabash Cannonball, the death wasn't attributed to the roller coaster. The boy suffered from an irregular heartbeat and the family chose not to pursue legal action against Opryland.

Hauntings

According to those who worked at Opryland the park was said to be an eerie place to work, especially at night. Park Rangers as well as other personnel that worked in the evenings often had experiences with faucets turning themselves on in the restrooms. Some also saw shadows darting around, especially in the New Orleans Area.

One former Ranger even claimed to have seen an old woman believed to be Mrs. McGavock one night after the park closed. In fact, the former security guard even told friends that he thought the lady was following him because she showed up wherever he went! Finally after he ran as fast as he could and screamed for help, the mysterious lady left him alone.

On another occasion late one night, a park employee was picking up trash by the Screamin' Delta Demon. As the young man was cleaning up, a very old lady approached him and asked, "Might I inquire as to what year this is?" Thinking it was some kind of prank, the staff member laughed and started to reply. But before he could say a word, the woman suddenly vanished right in front of him! The young man stopped what he was doing and called it a night.

Mrs. McGavock was really intrigued by the cleaning crews in the area. One night as employees were wrapping up, all of a sudden they saw a staff member sprinting through the park. When he finally got to safety he told his co-worker he was cleaning up at the Chicken

Plantation when an old woman casually floated up to him. Needless to say, that was his last night working in the park.

But Lady McGavock didn't just hang out in the New Orleans Area. It was her property. She could go anywhere she wanted. In fact, staff members would randomly see her walking around places like the El Paso Train Station and Opry Plaza after the sun had gone down.

"It was common for Security to be called to the gazebos at the entrance because a woman was seen after closing standing in them, "said Lincoln Head who worked in the park from 1982 and 1989.

Head never saw Mrs. McGavock but he likely had an experience with her one night in the children's area after the park had closed.

 "It was a little after 11p.m.," recalled Head. "I was driving my Cushman around to pick up trash from the service areas," said Head. "When I crossed over the train tracks near the rafts, the music stopped in the kiddie section. The music never stopped and never in just one area. I proceeded to the restroom to grab the bags left by the sweepers and heard a loud noise in the men's side. When I went in, I saw all the stall doors swinging violently back and forth. I never saw the Dark Lady, but I didn't stay long! I jumped back on my Cushman and left! When I crossed the tracks, the music came back on in the area. I was weirded out!

In retrospect, I do wish I had seen 'someone'. When I first started, the guys that had been there from the beginning all had a story about weird stuff but it seemed like it calmed down in the 90s."

While Lincoln Head didn't come face to face with Mrs. McGavock, Randy Smith who worked in the park for over 15 years did have a run in with the McGavock heiress late one night.

"Part of my routine involved riding throughout the park on a little Honda Trail 70," explained Smith. "One night I rode out the gate from the State Fair area onto the back service road next to the river, and there she was. She was dressed in white, not black. I didn't stop to chat. I made a quick U-turn and rode back into the park."

Even though Randy Smith didn't stop to say hello, he seemed to have piqued the interest of Mrs. McGavock. He had a few other interactions with her in the park.

"I was near the chicken plantation one night and I saw somebody looking through the fence," recalled Smith. "I thought it was one of my workers goofing off so I opened the gate and looked. Nobody was there. Another time I was walking through the western area one night and walked into an area where the temp dropped by probably 20-30 degrees. I kept walking and the temperature went back to normal (hot). So yeah, she is real."

Opry Mills

In November 1998 Opryland officials announced that they had signed a deal with their first anchor tenant for the new mall. Dave & Buster's, who was best known for their high tech simulation video games and carnival style amusements, would be occupying a large space on the north side of the mall. By bringing in a Chuck E. Cheese for grown-ups Gaylord let it be known that they weren't just targeting parents who needed to buy tennis shoes for their kids. Opry Mills was going to be a place where you could come spend the day, with or without children.

A short time later other retailers and restaurants that would be coming to Opry Mills began to leak out into the local papers. Bass Pro Shops, Tower Records, Rainforest

Café, Wolfgang Puck's Café and Alabama Grill International were all rumored to have signed leases. A new state of the art Regal Movie Theater with 18 screens and IMAX also was said to be interested in a space in the mall.

With Opry Mills officials working on securing tenants for the mall, crews worked all through 1998 and 1999 tearing down the theme park and repurposing the area for the mall. With flooding having been an issue in 1975, Gaylord put an emphasis on keeping water out of the mall should the Cumberland River overflow again. Dump trucks brought close to a million cubic feet of dirt in to raise the site 8 to 10 feet. With the ground elevated, crews poured the foundation in the Spring of 1999 then spent the summer working on the framework and roof.

That summer Gaylord announced that Opry Mills' Grand Opening would take place on May 12, 2000. A press conference was also held to announce the fourteen anchor tenants that would be occupying large spaces in the mall.

- Apple Barn Cider Barn and General Store
- Barnes and Nobles
- Bass Pro
- Bed Bath and Beyond
- Blacklion
- Gibson Bluegrass Showcase
- Jillians (Dave and Busters)
- NASCAR Silicon Motor Speedway

- Off 5th Saks Fifth Avenue Outlet
- Old Navy
- Rainforest Café
- Regal Cinemas
- Sun and Ski Sports
- Tower Records

With the anchors in place, Gaylord projected the new mall and its other 170 stores, restaurants and entertainment venues would draw 17 million people in the first twelve months.

On May 12, 2000 Opry Mills opened for business. Gaylord was conservative with their projections for the Grand Opening and only expected 10,000 to show up on a Friday with kids still in school. In fact, they even held a drawing and the first 5,000 shoppers had a chance to win one of ten $1,000 shopping sprees. However, more than 5,000 people came on opening day. Over 100,000 people came to Opry Mills on the first day to see what the new mall was all about. Women were blown away by the mall's fashion district that featured tall storefronts that rivaled the shopping experience you would get in New York City. Men were also equally impressed by the gargantuan Bass Pro Shops that resembled a rustic 155,000 square feet hunting lodge.

The new IMAX movie theater inside Regal was also a hit. Kids came from all over middle Tennessee to see a film about a computer animated dinosaur as well as a documentary about NBA legend Michael Jordan.

Opry Mills was very aggressive with promotions and events throughout May to entice people to come to the mall. Celebrities like Tennessee Titans football players, local radio personalities and characters from the kids' hit TV show Blue's Clues made appearances and did meet and greets.

For those who appreciated the arts, the Nashville Symphony also performed at the mall and local theatre groups did plays on some of the stages throughout Opry Mills.

Opry Mills was a hit. Although they didn't quite hit the projected 17million visitors in the first year, the new mall drew in 14 million people, which was seven times the number of visitors to Opryland.

Despite pushback from those who held a grudge after the theme park was torn down, the mall flourished in Nashville. On Black Friday in 2005, 85,000 shoppers visited the Opry Mills. That December the mall drew roughly the same number of visitors that went to the Opryland during the entire 1974 season.

In 2007 Opry Mills was acquired by Simon Property Group, a real estate investment firm in Indianapolis, Indiana. Even with new owners, the mall continued to flourish.

Piranhas?

As Opry Mills was getting ready for their tenth birthday bash in May 2010, a severe storm dumped 13 inches of rain in Nashville over a span of 6 hours. The Cumberland River crested more than 11 feet over flood levels and caused problems all around Nashville. The flood ultimately killed 26 people in the area and forced over 10,000 people from their homes.

Like the nearby Opry House and Opryland Hotel, Opry Mills was also affected by the rising waters. Yet, unlike the hotel that escaped with only some damage, Opry Mills was decimated. Bass Pro Shops was under two feet of water. The theater and other shops on the west side of the mall that were closest to the river had ten feet of water, some had slightly more.

As if the flood wasn't bad enough, word began to spread around Nashville that several piranhas with razor-sharp teeth managed to escape from the 200,000 gallon fish tank in the Aquarium Restaurant on the northeastern side of the mall. The restaurant's parent company insisted that no piranhas had escaped but still rumors persisted all over town for months after the flood. Even if the deadly tropical fish did manage to escape from the Aquarium Restaurant, they wouldn't be able to survive in the Cumberland River once temperatures dipped in the fall.

Once the flood waters subsided crews got to work cleaning out mold, redoing the floors and looking for piranhas. After a few months, work abruptly stopped when the insurance money dried up. The insurance companies claimed the mall was insured for $50 million and refused to pay for anything over that amount. However, Simon Property Group countered that they had documentation stating that they were insured for $200 million. Once the two groups reached an impasse, Opry Mills' parent company took 16 insurance companies to court in Davidson County.

However, Bass Pro Shops didn't sit around and wait on the attorneys. They rolled up their sleeves and got to work. Bass Pro's hard work resulted in them re-opening in October 2010. With Bass Pro Shops back in business, other stores like Dave and Buster's, Sun and Ski Sport, VF Outlet and the movie theater followed their lead and re-opened before Christmas.

As Opry Mills' case slowly made its way through the legal system the mall remained closed indefinitely. Opry Mills' executives did their best to calmly assure everyone that they were expecting to reopen in the spring of 2011. Unfortunately the gears of the justice system turned slow and rumors persisted that the mall wasn't profitable enough to merit reopening. Amongst all the uncertainty, Opry Mills issued a press release in April 2011 announcing that they had secured financing to repair and rebuild the mall. Opry Mills would be back in business in the spring of 2012.

After being closed for one year, ten months and 28 days, Opry Mills reopened on March 29, 2012. Mall officials held a ceremonial ribbon cutting that ended with confetti and streamers falling from the ceiling. The mall celebrated their Grand Re-opening with several different events, all of which culminated with a free Josh Turner concert in early May.

Since then Opry Mills has become the premier shopping destination in middle Tennessee. With the exception of a shooting in a hallway next to a pretzel business that left a local man dead in 2018, life has gone back to normal in the mall.

Lilly

As far back as the late 1990s while the mall was being built, construction workers talked amongst themselves about losing tools. From time to time tools or supplies workers were using would disappear only to be discovered scattered all over the floor somewhere else on the worksite. Today some of the same mischievous shenanigans are still taking place in Opry Mills.

While it is generally accepted amongst people who work in the mall that the shopping center is haunted by Mrs. McGavock, I ran into a few people who told me a very different story. According to them, the mall wasn't haunted before the flood. The paranormal activity began when a young lady named Lilly died in the flood in 2010. There are multiple versions of the story depending on who you talk to. Lilly was someone who either worked in the mall, lived nearby, or was a homeless person who came to the mall when it got too hot or too cold outside. Either way, something happened during the flood and Lilly's body was supposedly discovered in the parking lot after the water subsided.

With that being said, I can't find any record of a woman named Lilly dying in the 2010 flood. Twenty one people died in Middle Tennessee, but none of them were named Lilly. The only way the theory holds water (pun not intended) is if Lilly was homeless; and since there was no one to identify her body, it got swept under the rug. Even if you do make that stretch, a homeless woman that drowned still would've made headlines, even during the flood.

Maybe there is something to the Lilly story, but I'm just more inclined to believe it is Lady McGavock. She was also seen around Opryland on occasion. Why wouldn't she be making her rounds on the same piece of property she's still unhappy about?

353 Opry Mills Drive

At the trendy rainforest-themed restaurant in the south
end of the mall, staff members often come in sometimes
in the morning to find merchandise in the floor. While it's
laughed off as an animatronic fixture named "Tracy
Tree", paranormal activity is genuinely accepted by some
of those who work there.

Tracy Tree

"I feel like the whole mall is haunted," said one current employee. "It gets creepy here at night, a lot of that is because of the animatronics. Sometimes in the mornings we will find toys in the floor. We just say it's because of Tracy, even though she doesn't come on at night. Even if it came on, it shouldn't knock anything off the shelves."

349 Opry Mills Drive

Next door to the jungle-themed restaurant is a space that is presently home to a wine shop. While there are similar stories from this location, they don't necessarily come from the current tenants. While a staff member conceded that the hallways in the back of the mall can be "straight up nightmare" fuel at night, nothing has happened to him in the location.

However, when the space was rented out to a sporting goods store a few years ago, employees often had problems with electronics.

"Mrs. McGavock loved my security cameras and she played with the registers," claimed the former manager of the store. "The security monitor was in the back and she would play around with it and make it turn to static. We had someone test it and work on it but nothing was wrong with it. She was mischievous, never mean."

Juste Dylan who also worked in the location for over a year also had strange things happen when he was working.

"Spooky stuff would happen at night after we closed down. Lights would flicker and we'd hear strange noises", explained Dylan. "As weird as it was and sounds, we would even say something on our way out," explained Dylan. "We'd say 'Alright Mrs., we are leaving. Don't get too mad at us."

Oddly enough, Dylan and other employees in the store would often countdown their cash register and find that it was off by ten cents on numerous occasions. Each time they chalked it up to a playful Mrs. McGavock messing around with them and hiding a dime.

319 Opry Mills Drive

Just a few doors down in the location that is currently home to a high-end denim company, strange things have also been known to take place.

Staff members often hear loud noises and sometimes the sounds of screaming inside the space. However, Gemma Hardy who works in the store has a logical explanation. Many of the shops have open ceilings and sounds that come from 100 feet away could reverberate throughout many of the retail spaces inside the mall.

With the odd noises debunked, staff members can't explain why they find clothing in the floor in the mornings or why the security alarms randomly go off by the door when no one is around.

Whatever is going on in the store is enough to make Gemma Hardy second guess herself at night after the store has shut down for the day.

"There are some nights where at the end of the night I'll go through the fitting rooms and make sure everything is cleaned out of them," explained Hardy. "Then I'll come back and the fitting room curtains will be closed. Then it becomes one of those things where I thought that I did it, but maybe I didn't do it..."

375 Opry Mills Drive

As I worked on this project, I spoke to dozens of people who either work in the mall or had worked in the mall. The one store that kept getting brought up more than any other was the specialty gift shop on the south end of Opry Mills. From things jumping off the shelf to anomalies with the security cameras, weird things were commonplace in this location.

"One day when I worked there I turned the corner and one of the toys fell off the shelf," said Amanee Harris, a former employee. "Well, it didn't really fall. It was more like it jumped off the shelf and went about three feet."

When I spoke to a current staff member about the alleged paranormal activity inside the store, she acknowledged that it was something that was generally accepted inside the retail space.

"People have talked about it," said the employee. "You do hear noises in there all the time and we do find stuff in the floor quite often. And it's funny, when we have gone back to look at the cameras to see what happened, you will see the merchandise where it is supposed to be. Then it will skip a second. Then there is stuff in the floor."

Some of the merchandise that falls could have theoretically just fallen because a sticker that holds a plastic hook could have come off. But other more sturdy items that fall seem to have been raised over a lip on the edge of a hook.

"Sometimes some of the things that fall off, they fall off of pegs with a lip on it," said the employee. "There is no reason it should fall off and be in the floor when I come in early in the morning."

509 Opry Mills Drive

Over at the shoe store odd things have also been known to happen. One night after the mall had shut down; an associate walking out of the store felt something tug on her backpack. Noises inside the location are also commonplace but the oddest story I heard about the store pertained to a rack of Toms shoes on display.

"When we walked into the office all the shoes were on the rack," recalled Emily Summers, who works in the store. "When we came out, all of the shoes on one side of the rack were on the ground. It was only on one side! We were pretty freaked out."

515 Opry Mills Drive

One of the eeriest ghost stories comes from one of the strangest and coolest places in Opry Mills, the wax museum. Each night after the museum shuts down; a staff member mops their floors. Well, one night in 2017 after the floor had been mopped the associates noticed something odd.

"We have a room with really dark floors," explained a longtime employee. "We don't mop during the day because of the guests that come through, so we mop it after we close. About twenty minutes after it was mopped and the floor started to dry, they came back through and it looked like one or two bare feet had walked through. All of the employees have to wear closed toe shoes and the studio team has to wear boots because they work with heavy wax. It wasn't anyone who worked back there. We just always blamed it on Mrs. McGavock.

Compared to other stores in the mall, Mrs. McGavock, or whatever is in the mall, isn't very active in the museum. However, in June of 2020, after the mall reopened after the coronavirus pandemic something odd happened once everything had shut down for the night.

"We have a cork board by the office and break room," said the staff member. "There is a studio team that puts notes on it for what they have to do. As one of the studio artists was leaving, she was at the time clock, clocking out for the night and the board came off the door. But it didn't fall! It went horizontal down the hallway five or six feet. We caught it on the security footage. The door had been closed and it didn't cause it. She was the only one there."

539 Opry Mills Drive

The most active part of the mall seems to be the northern section of Opry Mills. Ironically enough, this section is in the vicinity of where The Screamin' Delta Demon, Flume Zoom and the Rock N Roller Coaster were located in the park. Strangely enough, the majority of the rides and attractions from the old theme park would've been located in what is now the parking lot of the mall.

The men and women's clothing store located on the north end of the mall has been known to have issues with the walkie talkies that employees use to communicate with each other.

"The walkie talkies will go off for no reason, said Crystal Cruz, who works in the store. "It can be sitting on the dock and it will start going off and it won't stop. We have to go turn it off. Then when we turn it back on, it won't go back off."

Like other locations in the mall, staff members also hear strange noises from time to time.

"Sometimes in the stock room, I'll hear things but that could come from the store next door," said Cruz. "But there will be times after closing when no one is in the store and I'll hear a sound like someone is rattling a hanger."

570 Opry Mills Drive

If you are going to have a haunted wax museum, you have to have a haunted movie theater, right? Employees at the theater have claimed to hear odd noises such as footsteps walking around in the lobby after all the customers have left for the night. One staff member also told me that they have seen shadows and what they thought there were people walking out of the corner of their eyes. Each time they turned around no one was there.

Several years ago Opry Mills had a rock climbing attraction set up by the movie theater. Apparently Mrs. McGavock was very intrigued by the structure and the people climbing it.

"My daughter was doing the rock climb," explained Linda Bartee, who was visiting from out of town. "She was about 9 and really good at it. It was the middle of the day and there was a crowd at the window watching her. I saw this elderly woman staring at her in shock. She looked petrified. I turned my eyes for a split second and there was no old lady.

She was solid in appearance and had on black, although I could only see her from her chest up. She stood out to me because she was open mouthed staring like she was taken aback. I guess being from that era she would consider it improper for a little girl. Combine that with a look of fear. I guess mortified would be the right term to use."

Opryland Hotel

In early 1972, as Opryland was getting ready to open, officials from the National Life and Accident Insurance Company and WSM began kicking around plans for a 200 room motor lodge called "Oprytowne".

The new motel was to be located on 25 acres to the north of the new theme park, just off of Briley Parkway. However, once Opryland was open, officials started to realize that any type of facility should not just cater to those coming to the area for the theme park or the future Opry House. Convention space would be crucial to fill up the rooms in cold winter months when Opryland wouldn't be open. With a convention center, "Oprytowne" would be in demand year round, instead of just the spring and summer when tourists came to Opryland.

The plans for the motel gradually morphed into a larger upscale hotel with a large convention center that was scheduled to open in July 1973. The plans were ultimately pushed back a few years as Opryland officials decided to go much bigger on 30 acres just north of the park.

Two local architecture firms were hired to design a 614 room hotel with 90,000 square feet of meeting and exhibit space. Architects-Engineers Associates of Nashville was hired to design the main building of the hotel. Another group led by local architect Earl Swennson was hired to design the hotel as well as the exterior that was designed to resemble the Governor's Palace in Williamsburg, Virginia.

Five free-standing buildings were built around a three story core building that contained a lobby, restaurants, shops and a ball room that had the capacity to seat 2,200 people.

Word quickly spread about the Opryland Hotel in Nashville as well as around the country, and before ground was even broken in April 1976, eleven conventions had been booked in the new facility.

Originally it was believed that the hotel would be completed in November 1977, but some bad weather that winter put that grand opening in jeopardy. Even though weather kept workers off the worksite in January and February, additional crews were brought in during the spring. Despite the hiccups, the Opryland Hotel management insisted that not only would the hotel open in November as planned; they would actually begin receiving guests in August. Ultimately, they were a little too ambitious and the Opryland Hotel moved their opening back to late November as originally planned.

The new hotel was unlike anything Nashville had ever seen and was the largest convention center in the state of Tennessee at the time. The Opryland Hotel used a state of the art Honeywell Delta 1000 Energy Conservation System to heat and cool the hotel. By 1970s standards, using computers to regulate the temperature in the hotel was very high tech. And with 10 acres of carpeting, over 44,0080 sheets, 44,000 towels and washcloths, 864 telephones, 6,046 chairs, 1,281 tables, 1,113 miles of wiring, the Opryland Hotel was colossal compared to other hotels around middle Tennessee.

The Opryland Hotel contained 614 rooms, 54 of which were suites, the prices ranged from $24 to $250 for a night in the lavish hotel.

With the hotel's grand opening scheduled for November 26, 1977 hotel management opened the doors of the new facility the day before to invite locals in to check things out. Roughly two hundred people walked in to inspect the Magnolia Lobby and its three-story vaulted ceiling and grand staircase. The locals also got the first peek at the beauty salon, jewelry store, women's and men wear shops, antique store, gift shop, specialty food shop and car rental stand that was available to the hotel's guests.

The hotel held its Grand Opening a few weeks later on December 19. Minnie Pearl and other Opry stars as well as local politicians and board members from National Life all attended the event to kick things off for the new hotel.

A few days later, the first event in the hotel was a "Grand Old Party" when the Tennessee Republican party held a lavish dinner in the hotel. The Republican's brought in conservative entertainers Roy Acuff, Chet Atkins, Eddy Arnold and Jerry Reed to play for over 1,400 Republicans from all over the state who descended upon the hotel for the event.

The same weekend the hotel held its first convention. The American Contract Bridge League held a regional tournament in the hotel that featured over 800 Bridge players from all 50 states that came to Music City to play cards over the weekend.

For New Years the hotel offered different packages featuring brunch, dinner and dancing to entice people to come spend New Year's Eve in the hotel. In fact, with the Republicans already having an event in the hotel, the Tennessee Democratic Party had to get in on the fun too. The Democrats held an extravagant gala at the hotel on New Year's Eve.

Politicians and the hotel would be a running theme throughout the years. In 1979 Vice President Walter Mondale spoke at an event to raise money for President Jimmy Carter's re-election campaign. Naturally, their opposition for the White House also held an event in the hotel the following year. Republican Presidential nominee Ronald Reagan appeared at the hotel while on the campaign trail. The former Hollywood star-turned politician was the guest of honor at a $250 a plate dinner to raise money for his campaign.

Over the years other prominent politicians such as Vice President Al Gore and President Bill Clinton attended fundraising events in the hotel.

In 1979 Opryland officials purchased 57 acres from a local businessman to expand the park and hotel. Over the next nine years the hotel expanded not once, but twice.

In 1983 the hotel completed its first major expansion by adding 467 rooms as well as 30,000 square feet of ballroom space. The most jaw dropping new feature was the 150 foot tall glass enclosed Victorian Garden Conservatory. The new conservatory was put together with 2,700 large glass panels that were carefully put into place by a helicopter and construction crews. Once completed, the Garden Conservatory featured a sprawling two acre tropical garden with 6,000 tropical plants such as banana, orange and coffee trees as well as running streams, waterfalls, fountains, rock gardens, and an art gallery.

Five years later the hotel added more exhibition space, five new shops and 1,216 more rooms. With 1,891 rooms, a new 24 hour check in station was also added to help the guests check in quicker.

A second atrium called "The Cascades" was also added to complement the Garden Conservatory. The Cascades featured two more acres of ponds and waterfalls and included a new restaurant that was surrounded by lush gardens that overlooked a giant waterfall.

But Opryland officials weren't done growing yet. With occupancy at 20% above the national levels, the hotel expanded again in the mid-90s. 4.5 acres were acquired for another expansion that at the time was the largest construction project in the history of Nashville. The fourth expansion saw the addition of the Delta wing of the hotel. The Delta wing included a new atrium, 1,000 new rooms, ten meeting rooms, a large ball room and a river ride. The new wing that was designed to reflect the architectural styles of New Orleans doubled the size of the already giant hotel.

In the early 2000s the Opryland Hotel was officially renamed "The Gaylord Opryland Resort and Convention Center". However, those in Nashville still referred to the hotel as "The Opryland Hotel". After the hotel was rebranded, the hotel underwent a $5 million renovation that included improvements to rooms as well as restaurants, bars and shops.

After three major expansions in its first twenty years, the Opryland Hotel didn't grow in the first decade of the 21st century. There were rumors about a large amphitheater that was to be built on the property but it never materialized. Even though a new atrium wasn't on the horizon, hotel officials were working on additional projects to keep the Opryland Hotel as one of the premier hotel and convention destinations in the country.

In 2011 the hotel opened an Event Center where the annual Christmas event "Ice" is now held each year. Visitors can enjoy ice sculptures as well as riding down a two story ice slide during Christmastime.

Seven years later, the hotel added an upscale three story indoor water park called Soundwaves. Featuring traditional water park attractions like water slides, a wave pool, rapid and lazy river rides and a surfing simulator, the attraction also had an outdoor pool complete with a large theater screen. With hundreds of palm trees and exotic plants, waterlogged guests could also enjoy relaxing around the indoor pools where it was kept at a balmy 84 degrees year round.

Soundwaves was a hit with guests. Yet, it didn't sit too well with locals who wanted to go to the water park. Seeing the opportunity, Gaylord officials created a package that offered discounted rates to the water park and an overnight stay for Tennesseans as well as another package with a steeper discount for Davidson County residents. At times locals could also purchase day passes during non-peak times for a reduced price.

Tragedy in the Hotel

On the night of Friday, October 5, 2001 hotel staff found the bodies of a married couple, Torre and Misty Norman lying on a concrete sidewalk in the Cascades Conservatory. Initially it was believed that the couple visiting from Hopkinsville, Kentucky got drunk after a long night in the hotel and began fighting. Allegedly, in a fit of rage, Torre's hot temper got the best of him and he pushed his wife off of the balcony in their room.

After calming down and realizing what he had done, Torre decided to end it all. Stricken with guilt and grief he climbed over the railing and plummeted five stories to the ground next to the remains of his wife. However, the fall didn't instantly kill Torre and he was transported to a nearby hospital where he clung to life for several hours before finally succumbing to his injuries.

As authorities began investigating the case, they found that it wasn't a simple murder-suicide. Based on the Metro Medical Examiner's findings, Misty Norman had been murdered and Torre Norman died accidently from a fall when he tried to cover up his crime. According to their theory, in a fit of rage, Torre strangled his wife in the hotel. After realizing what he had done, Torre decided to throw his wife's body over the fifth floor balcony to make it look like she had committed suicide. Unfortunately, as he was lifting Misty's body over the railing, he lost his balance and fell roughly seventy feet to the walkway below. Whether it was a suicide or an accident, we will never really know.

Strangely enough, the story doesn't end there. In 2003 footage of Misty Norman's body in a Nashville morgue as well as the scene of her death, aired on the TLC show "True Stories from the Morgue". Infuriated by the invasion of privacy, Mrs. Norman's family sued the show's production company, as well as several other parties that were involved. The case never went to trial and a settlement was reached out of court that resulted in the show being abruptly canceled by the network.

Two and a half years later on July 20, 2004 a pipe bomb planted in an SUV detonated in an outer construction parking lot that was being used by the hotel. The only victim was a local man named William Young who was in the vehicle at the time. Young was suffering from depression and had been going through a hard time after recently filing for bankruptcy.

Desperate and seeing no way out, Young told family and friends that someone was trying to kill him and allegedly shot a bullet hole into his own car to prove how dangerous things had gotten. A short time later the despondent man signed a living will and concocted a story about finding a job in Nicaragua and told his family goodbye. Before driving to the Opryland Hotel to kill himself with the bomb, Young mailed a letter to his wife informing her of a $1 million life insurance policy.

The explosion was felt over a mile away and only the shell of Young's vehicle remained.

The Flood

On May 1st and 2nd, 2010 a massive storm rolled into Nashville dumping 13 to 16 inches of rain in middle Tennessee. As the Cumberland River began to rise, the water eventually breached the levees and began pouring into the Cascades lobby that sat at the lowest elevation of any point in the hotel. With Cascades under 15 feet of water, approximately 1,500 guests as well as 500 employees were evacuated to higher ground.

Even though flood water filled roughly 1/5 of the hotel, only a few of the hotel's 2,881 rooms received any water damage.

Once the water subsided, hotel officials assessed the $170 million in damages and got to work cleaning up and rebuilding the hotel. With the hotel closed, Gaylord began a $270 million facelift on the property with some much needed restorations and renovations.

In mid-November the hotel began receiving guests, just in time for the annual Country Christmas festivities. With the hotel reopened, Gaylord spent $1.5 million in advertising and an additional $7 million on wining and dining bloggers, journalists and travel industry professionals in hopes of spreading the word that they were back in business. The plan worked and the rooms quickly began selling out.

Hauntings

One of the worst kept secrets at the Opryland Hotel is the legend of Mary Louise McGavock, or as she is known around the hotel, "Lady McGavock" or "Mrs. McGavock." Hotel staff members talk about it openly and typically blame any kind of strange occurrences on the lady who had the hotel built on her property.

"I worked 3rd shift at the hotel and I mostly saw her in the ballrooms," recalled a former security guard. "The times I saw her, she was in an older style dress. Most of the time, I only got a glimpse of her from the corner of my eye. You would just feel like someone was watching you and would catch her on stage in the ballrooms."

But Mrs. McGavock didn't just hang out in the ballrooms. She's also been known to linger in the restrooms and play with the faucets while staff members were using the facilities.

"One night a friend of mine was in one of the restrooms standing at a urinal," continued the former security guard. "All the faucets started turning themselves on one by one. He walked out and quit."

Cathy Smith who has worked in the hotel for five years has also had some strange experiences in the restrooms. "I've been in some of the restrooms washing my hands and the faucet all the way on the other side will turn itself on, and then turn itself off.

Typically, most of the stories about Mrs. McGavock tend to come from the Magnolia wing, which is the original part of the resort. Longtime staff members tell stories about elevators that never seemed to work right as well as lights not just turning themselves off and on, but disassembling themselves so they would stop working altogether.

Several years ago the brass, 18 foot tall chandelier in the Magnolia lobby suddenly stopped working. After workers took the 1,000 pound three-tier light fixture down with a crane, they found that all the connections inside the chandelier had somehow been mysteriously taken apart thirty feet in the air. Once the crew reattached all the connections, the chandelier began working once again.

According to those who have worked in the hotel, the chandelier has also been known to move on its own and slowly rock back and forth on occasion.

Celeste Crim, who was part of the hotel's paratransit service not only had a strange experience in the Magnolia lobby, she actually came face to face with Mrs. McGavock one evening in the Magnolia lobby.

"I was there to pick up a passenger for my last pickup around 6 PM," recalled Crim. "So I walk in the Magnolia entrance and see this woman in all black walk in front of me. I was scanning the area looking for my passenger and didn't think anything of it until I glanced back where the woman in black should have been. She was gone. There was three seconds in between me seeing her and looking for her. There was nowhere for her to go. No one else seemed to be phased by her appearing and disappearing, but I didn't ask.

There was a woman sitting in a chair and we made eye contact, but she never averted her eyes to look at the woman in black in front of me. I had to stop in the middle of a step to keep from walking into this apparition!"

Another former employee who also saw Mrs. McGavock in the Magnolia wing was Virginia McCabe. According to McCabe, while working room service one night, not only did she see Lady McGavock, but she also saw the Lady in Black near one of the Presidential suites surrounded by an eerie green mist!

"The old part of the hotel was so creepy at night," said McCabe. "I have seen the green mist and it would always be moving and it felt as though someone was walking with me! It seemed saddened and a heavy feeling was on your heart."

Another current staff member I spoke to also reiterated that the Magnolia wing is the most haunted part of the hotel. Even though she hasn't seen Mrs. McGavock, she definitely believes the rumors.

"The Magnolia section, which is the oldest part of the hotel, is haunted by the ghost of Mrs. McGavock," explained the associate. "We have speakers in the ballrooms and one day when I was in there, you could hear them buzzing. All of a sudden, I heard a loud pop and all the lights came on! Anyone who has worked in the hotel long enough has a story. I've not seen her but I've had a lot of experiences with her messing around with the lights and stuff."

Sonya Curtis Brinton worked in the hotel for sixteen years. While the former longtime associate never saw Mrs. McGavock, she experienced a lot of strange things that she chalked up to the mysterious phantom.

"I was there 16 years and never saw her," said Brinton. I did have some strange things happen in my office that couldn't be explained from time to time though.

Things went missing. I had a bunch of Opryland park souvenir memorabilia I kept in my office on the bookshelf. From time to time, they would be moved. It was like someone was looking at them, and then set them back in a different spot. I had a picture from the Grizzly River Rampage come up missing, and then it was back a couple months later."

But things didn't just come up missing or get moved around; the Lady in Black would also leave things in the office that didn't belong there.

"Odd things would show up that wasn't mine," continued Brinton. "I locked my office door when I left, and one morning I came into find a cup of lukewarm coffee on my desk. Sometimes I would just unlock my door in the morning and have a feeling someone had been there. It scared me at first. Security even brought in a clock radio that was somehow rigged with a camera to my office. It had a motion detector so they could see if someone was coming in, but we didn't see anything while it was being monitored. The only people who had keys to my office were myself and my boss. We didn't know how anyone could've gotten in. We didn't even have housekeeping coming to clean during that time anymore so we knew it wasn't them.

Some of the guys I worked with told me stories of similar things and they also blamed it on Mrs. McGavock."

As I talked to former hotel staff about the ghostly sightings, the one place that kept getting mentioned was the fireplace by the Hermitage meeting rooms in the old Magnolia wing. According to them, Mrs. McGavock had been spotted by the fireplace on numerous occasions by hotel security. The sightings seemed to be more frequent in 2010 when the hotel was shut down for several months after the flood.

In addition to the strange activity that is often attributed to Mrs. McGavock, I talked to a handful of current and former employees that always felt uneasy in the Grand Nashville Lobby.

The walls in the lobby are painted to depict scenes from the 19th century in Nashville. Max Hochstetler, an associate professor of art at Austin Peay was commissioned to paint 2,700 square feet of murals when the hotel was being built. Hochstetler painted recognizable places such as the old Public Square, Ryman Auditorium, Union Station and other prominent landmarks from the time period in 1977 and again in 1980.

The uneasiness the staff members felt in the Grand Nashville Lobby stems from the characters that are in the murals. In all there are 99 people ranging from children to adults. In fact, the artist even painted some of his family members as well as himself in the mural. Whoever they are, those who have worked in that part of the hotel talk about being watched by the people in the scenes, especially the children.

"I hated going back there at night," exclaimed one former employee. "I could be over by the stairs and I'd look up and see one of the guys in the painting look directly at me. Or thirty minutes or so later, I could be walking out of the ballroom and glance over, then boom! He's staring right at me again. It didn't matter where you were. It always seemed like some of them were always watching you."

While I worked on this project I consulted with a Sumner County empath I had worked with on some of my previous books. Over the years she has told me a number of things about various haunted places in middle Tennessee that I have taken her to. In each instance, not only was she right, but she also had no business knowing about the things she was talking about. She had only been to the hotel on two occasions and wasn't aware of the legend of Mary Louise McGavock.

When I asked her if she ever sensed anything in the hotel she mentioned that she picked up on the presence of a widow. Yet, she also sensed a Native American presence and mentioned that there were apparitions of energy replaying on the property.

Strangely enough, out of the blue she mentioned that she thought suicides had occurred in the hotel. Without knowing anything about the history of the hotel and its property, the empath went 3 for 3 with her assessment.

Music Valley Drive

Originally known as Elzie Miller Road, the road across the street from the Opryland Hotel was home to a large chunk of property that was developed in the 1970s.

As the theme park caught on, restaurants, hotels and other tourist attractions began to pop up on McGavock Pike and the newly-christened "Music Valley Drive". After Opryland U. S. A. closed, many of the businesses dried up, although some have managed to stay and draw in customers from the Grand Ole Opry House, Opry Mills and the hotel.

2406 Music Valley Drive

After the first Cracker Barrel opened in 1969 in nearby Lebanon, Tennessee, the old-timey restaurant and gift shop became so popular that they began opening other stores around the middle Tennessee area. One of those early locations was the store on Music Valley Drive that was built in 1977.

According to employees in the store, the restaurant is not haunted by Mrs. McGavock or Native Americans. The spirit in the old country store is that of a friendly old soul named "Uncle Herschel", the real-life uncle of the founder of Cracker Barrel and the namesake of a popular breakfast meal served in the restaurant.

When I visited the location and talked to a cashier about the alleged hauntings in the business she immediately started laughing.

"Is it haunted," asked the cashier. "I don't believe in ghosts but they say that it is. There's a story that has been going around about it being Uncle Herschel's ghost. This was one of the first Cracker Barrel's so we think it's Uncle Herschel. We will be standing at the register and something random will fall off a shelf and no one will be near it. Anytime something falls off the shelf, someone will say, 'Uncle Herschel strikes again!'"

While the playful entity in the store may or may not be everyone's favorite uncle, another longtime staff member told me, it's likely someone else.

"We've had two people pass away in the building in the past 30 years. One was an older gentleman who had a heart attack at the table. Another was an employee who was found dead in the bathroom."

While the associate didn't necessarily agree on the identity of the spirit, she does believe that there is something strange going on in the building.

"Oh it's haunted," said the associate. One night there was an employee in the building after hours. He started hearing voices and took off running out of the emergency exit. I've never seen anything myself but there are some stories."

2408 Music Valley Drive

A short distance from Cracker Barrel you will find the most popular sports bar in the area, Scoreboard Bar & Grill. While talking with people who worked around Music Valley Drive I heard that the sports bar was also haunted. So naturally I stopped in one afternoon to see if it was true.

When I walked into the establishment I was greeted by Jenny Hunt, who was fairly new at the time. As soon as I mentioned anything about ghosts I got an immediate and unexpected response from the young lady.

"Do you see the hair on my arms standing up," asked Jenny. "I had only been there for a few weeks but one morning around ten and I was opening. I walked through (to the bar area) and I heard what sounded like a breath or a huff. But there was no one there. I still get chills thinking about it."

Perhaps it was an isolated incident because all the other associates I spoke with had never seen or heard anything strange in the building.

2410 Music Valley Drive

In 1975 The Fiddlers Inn opened a few months before the Opryland Hotel. The hotel was extremely popular during that time and expanded two years later.

Like other establishments in the area, the hotel's popularity began to wane after Opryland closed down. In 2010 a man was found shot to death in the parking lot and ten years later another man was found dead on the sidewalk after a drug deal went bad.

As I worked on this project I ran into someone who had worked in the hotel over the years. According to them, they would see shadows moving around in a hallway in the inn. Sometimes they would also see lights on in vacant rooms. Even stranger, they sometimes heard voices talking in them too!

In early 2021 I visited the hotel and talked with an associate about some of the alleged paranormal activity in the area. Ironically enough, when I brought up the shadows that I had been told about, one of the staff members jokingly asked me if I wanted to take a ghost tour of the old hotel.

"I haven't seen shadows," claimed the staff member. "You hear something sometimes, but I just brush it off. It's just noises. I was in the laundry room in the basement one day and I started hearing noises. It was really eerie and I could've sworn someone was in there with me. But, when I turned around, I didn't see anybody. It's weird things like that."

2416 Music Valley Drive

Tucked away in a shopping center behind the Fiddler's Inn is a shopping center that was built in the 1990s. One of the key tenants in the shopping center was the Ernest Tubb Record Shop, a business that was started by country music legend Ernest Tubb. However as CDs slowly went away and the recording industry went to streaming and digital, the store was forced to shut down in 2016. Today the location is home to a trendy gift shop that has something you won't find anywhere, Ernest Tubb's tour bus!

When the strip mall was built, the old record shop was built around Tubb's 1964 Silver Eagle "Green Hornet" tour bus that the legendary performer used from 1970 to 1979. It was believed that fans would be intrigued to see how life was on the road for musicians and would want to see Tubb's bus that he took to 48 states.

Tubb was a pioneer-of-sorts for country music performers. He, along with his band, the Texas Troubadours were the very first performers to travel the country to play in various towns. In fact, when Tubb needed a drummer in the 1960s, he hired Jack Green, not for his drumming ability, but because he needed a driver and someone with experience working as a mechanic.

Even though Ernest Tubb died in 1984, some say that the Country Music Hall of Famer may still be hanging out on his old tour bus. In fact, it wasn't a secret that when Tubb wasn't touring, he would often be found sleeping in the back of his bus that was parked behind his house. After so many years on the road, the singer had grown accustomed to sleeping in the vehicle.

Today people that work in the gift shop tell strange stories about hearing noises coming from the bus, and in some cases, people talking inside it when the store isn't open.

"There are rumors the bus is haunted," said Marissa Shriner, who works in the shop. "The previous owner had the bus completely blocked off and covered up. She didn't like it and said the bus was bad. People have said they've heard voices in it. It's also been known to get hot and cold in there, but it does have its own AC unit."

While visiting the store one afternoon I did an impromptu investigation on the bus. I did get some minor EMF fluctuations on my EMF meter inside the bus, but that could possibly be explained by bad wiring inside the old bus. I also got some strange sounds on my digital recorder but after talking to store personnel, I believe that may stem from some music that may have been playing inside the tour bus.

Last year Tubb's bus was purchased as part of a collection and supposedly it will be removed sometime in the future.

"They've attempted to remove the bus several times over the past 30 years, but couldn't get it out," said Shriner. "But how do you get it out?

The building was built around the bus to start with. It originally had an engine in it when they put it in, but the chemicals inside it caused a bunch of people to get sick. They had to pull it out, and then push it back in. To get the bus out they would have to take the front of the building. There have been contractors looking at it and they will probably have to take it out through the ceiling."

2611 McGavock Pike

Hoping to piggyback off the success of Opryland U. S. A.,
country music star Jerry Reed opened a dinner
theater/nightclub across the street from the Opryland
Hotel in 1977. Reed's Nashville Palace quickly became
the place in Nashville to have dinner and watch a show
featuring up and coming artists like Alan Jackson and
Lorrie Morgan as well as established stars like Mel Tillis.

But some of the best singers weren't on stage; they were
in the back washing dishes! In the early 1980s an aspiring
country singer named Randy Traywick moved to
Nashville to get a record deal. Unfortunately things

didn't work out for him so he took a job at the Nashville Palace working as a dishwasher. To pass the time Randy would often sing in the back while he worked. His fellow co-workers were blown away by Randy's voice and eventually he got permission to sing on stage. The young performer was a hit and eventually became a regular and eventually recorded a demo in the Palace. That demo got him a record deal with Warner Brothers, but there were some strings attached. Executives thought Randy Traywick wasn't a marketable name and asked the singer to change his name to Randy Travis. Randy signed the contract and quickly became a household name with hits like *Diggin' Up Bones* and *Forever and Ever, Amen*.

Like other businesses in the area, the Palace struggled to make money once Opryland closed and eventually shut down. However, the historic venue was revived a short time later and relocated to the old Stars Valley Expo Building a few doors down.

Today the Palace is still going strong. On Friday and Saturday night it is the place to go in the area to catch tomorrow's legends today.

As you would expect, the Nashville Palace is also haunted. But if you are looking for Lady McGavock, you're going to be disappointed. Former employees claim that the place is haunted by an unruly phantom that they have affectionately named "Leroy."

"I can't tell you how he got his name," said Tara Bebber who used to be the Director of Operations of the Palace and spent many late nights in the building. "It's believed that he's likely a Civil War soldier because when you catch a glimpse of him, he's wearing what appears to be a Confederate hat and coat. The hat is more of the "cowboy" style hat".

Leroy seems to enjoy the music that is played in the Palace. In fact, there are videos on YouTube that show orbs moving around on stage while Daryle Singletary and Rhonda Vincent were performing at the Palace. According to Tara, he was also captured walking across the stage on video one night while Larry Hamilton was performing.

But Leroy isn't there just for the music; he can be quite playful and mischievous as well. Leroy has been known to pull earrings out of ears and throw them and sometimes chase staff members down the hallway with his loud, thundering footsteps. More than one employee has told me that they have literally run out of the building late at night because of strange experiences that shook them up.

After so many odd things kept happening some of the employees did a paranormal investigation in the Palace.

"We had a ghost hunt one night in the back room and saw Leroy's legs materialize," exclaimed Tara. "He also said the name of one of our employees through a ghost hunting app.

What's strange is that he said a guy's first name, and then said his middle name at the exact moment the employee walked up to the piano we were all sitting around. The employee came over to join us and put his hand on the piano and the app said 'Jason', which isn't an uncommon name. But then immediately after, it said "Lewis", which is Jason's middle name.

Cursed

As I researched the area around Opryland, one thing jumped out at me about Music Valley Drive and Briley Parkway; there was an extraordinary amount of car accidents. In fact, in the early 1970s, as soon as Opryland opened and Briley Parkway was expanded, southbound motorists that were either impaired or driving too fast, began wrecking as soon as they went over the bridge over the Cumberland River.

In the late 1970s, after a string of deadly crashes, police set up extra patrols on that part of Briley Parkway to discourage people from speeding. But the police couldn't monitor the area 24/7 and people still kept crashing. In 1983, 1984 and 1985, that part of Briley Parkway averaged at least one death each year after a car hopped the median and ran headfirst into an oncoming car.

Ironically, one afternoon I was talking to Eli Geery, a local historian about Opryland, and the alleged hauntings. As we were discussing Music Valley Drive, Eli mentioned that his father worked in the area and that he along with others sometimes talked about Briley Parkway being cursed due to all the wrecks over the years.

"Back in the 1980s on Briley Parkway, just past the river, there's an embankment that curves when you go over the bridge," explained Geery. "They straightened it out in the 80s quite a bit, but there's still a little embankment in front of the campgrounds. It caused a lot of wrecks. It was so bad that they came in and resurveyed it because the grading was off. They had to redo it."

As a child Geery saw a gruesome accident on Briley Parkway that involved a truck driver that fell asleep in that exact spot. The truck went across the divider and went airborne into a truck on the other side of the road.

"It was like something out of the Dukes of Hazzard," exclaimed Geery. "She was driving one of the old 70s Ford's F150 pickup trucks. He hit the embankment, went airborne and took the cab right off the truck. The guy in the truck survived but it took the lady's head off and spit it out of the side. It rolled for what seemed like forever.

We sat there for two hours while they cleared it. The head sat there forever while everything was closed down. It took about two hours before a firefighter walked over and put the head in a bag. I couldn't take my eyes off of it."

After the city got Briley Parkway figured out, a new problem started to present itself nearby.

In between the campgrounds and a cluster of restaurants on Music Drive, there is a dimly-lit stretch of straightway adjacent to Briley Parkway that became the spot where kids would go drag racing on Friday nights. In the wintertime, when the campgrounds had shut down for the season, this part of Music Valley Drive was basically no man's land for teenagers who wanted to race. However, after several brutal crashes, the police began to actively patrol the area and the racing stopped.

In 1991, country music star Dottie West was involved in a horrific accident on Briley Parkway that sent shockwaves through Nashville. After her car had broken down on Harding Place, Dottie was running late for an appearance on the Grand Ole Opry. As she was sitting on the side of the road, George Thackston, her 81 year old neighbor saw her stranded and offered her a ride. Already running late,

Dottie told George to step on it. Unbeknownst to the performer, her neighbor had been drinking earlier in the evening and wasn't in any condition to be operating a vehicle.

As George flew like a bat out of hell down Briley Parkway to get the country star to the Opry, he couldn't slow down once he hit the off ramp. George and Dottie went airborne and came down crashing into the median.

While George walked away from the accident with injuries to his arm and back, Dottie suffered a ruptured spleen and a lacerated liver. Yet, since her injuries weren't visible, Dottie opted to not go to the hospital. When she realized her injuries were severe, it was too late; she died on the operating table from internal bleeding.

Even with all the accidents and death on Briley Parkway and Music Valley Drive, I don't necessarily think the roads are cursed. Poor planning by city officials and poor decisions by motorists are likely to blame for the crashes.

But then again, anytime you build anything on Native American land, old plantations or an angry widow's property, I suppose anything is possible.

If you'd like to learn more about the history and hauntings of Downtown Nashville, please check out Southern Ghost Stories: Downtown Nashville.

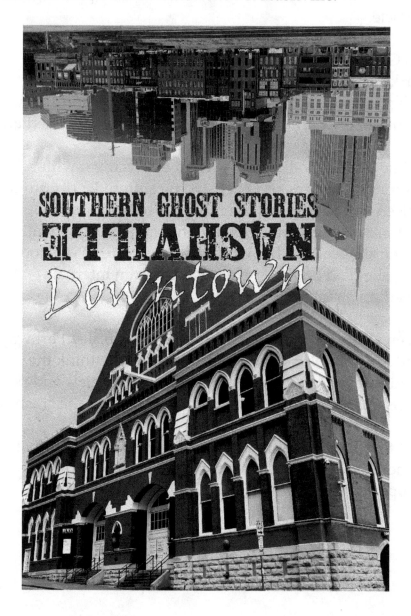

Also, please check out our other books Southern Ghost Stories: Ghosts of Gallatin, Murfreesboro, Spirits of Stones River, South Nashville and Haunted Hotels available at select retailers and Amazon.com. Also, be sure to follow Southern Ghost Stories on Instagram and Facebook.

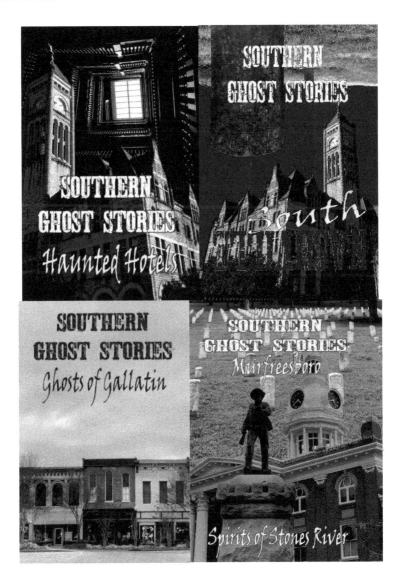

CPSIA information can be obtained
at www.ICGtesting.com
Printed in the USA
LVHW080254100723
751979LV00007B/574